Contents

About this Book

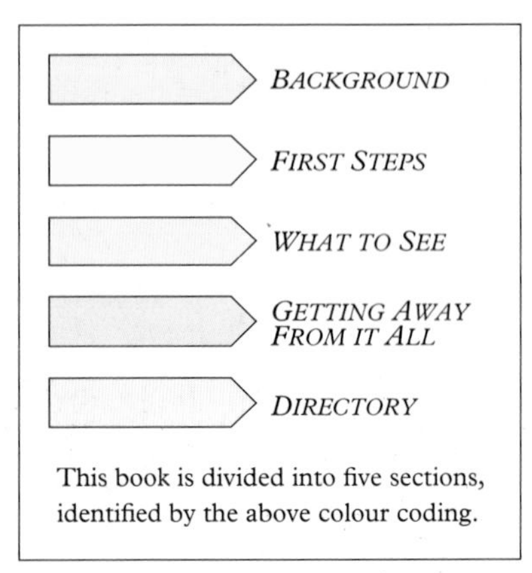

This book is divided into five sections, identified by the above colour coding.

Background gives an introduction to the Caribbean – its history, geography, politics, culture.

First Steps offers practical advice on arriving and getting around.

What to See is a alphabetical listing of places to visit, divided into the geographically arranged islands, interspersed with walks and tours.

Getting Away From it All highlights places off the beaten track where it is possible to relax and enjoy peace and quiet.

Finally, the ***Directory*** provides practical information – from shopping and entertainment to children and sport, including a section on business matters.

Special highly illustrated ***features*** on specific aspects of the region appear throughout the book.

Trunk Bay, US Virgin Islands

INCLUDING
BARBADOS & TRINIDAD

EASTERN CARIBBEAN

BY
NEIL MACLEAN

Produced by AA Publishing

Written by Neil Maclean

Original photography by Peter Baker

Edited, designed and produced by AA Publishing. Maps © The Automobile Association 1994

Distributed in the United Kingdom by AA Publishing, Fanum House, Basingstoke, Hampshire, RG21 2EA.

The contents of this publication are believed correct at the time of printing. Nevertheless, the publishers cannot accept responsibility for any errors or omissions, or for changes in the details given in this guide or for the consequences of any reliance on the information provided by the same. Assessments of attractions, hotels, restaurants and so forth are based upon the author's own experience and, therefore, descriptions given in this guide necessarily contain an element of subjective opinion which may not reflect the publishers' opinion or dictate a reader's own experiences on another occasion.
We have tried to ensure accuracy in this guide, but things do change and we would be grateful if readers would advise us of any inaccuracies they may encounter.

A CIP catalogue record for this book is available from the British Library.

ISBN 0 7495 0689 X

Published by AA Publishing (a trading name of Automobile Association Developments Limited, whose registered office is Fanum House, Basingstoke, Hampshire RG21 2EA. Registered number 1878835) and the Thomas Cook Group Ltd.

Colour separation: Daylight Colour Art PTE Ltd, Singapore

Printed by Edicoes ASA, Oporto, Portugal

Cover picture: *Pigeon Point, Tobago*
Title page: *Admiralty Bay, Bequia, Grenadines*
Above: *island boy, St Vincent*

BACKGROUND

'These green slopes, hemmed in by their Garden of Eden forests, have an almost miraculous beauty.'

PATRICK LEIGH FERMOR

Guadeloupe (1951)

Introduction

There is hardly an island in the Eastern Caribbean that has not been referred to as Paradise at some time or another on its advertising posters and colour brochures; but one man's Paradise is another man's unholy Purgatory.

Fortunately the truth is Paradise, or at least the holiday-away-from-the-office version of it which most of us seek from two weeks in the Caribbean, actually comes in as a many different flavours as there are drinks on a Barbados cocktail list at Happy Hour. The trick is to find out which one makes us happy.

There are some 40 islands in this book, not counting tiny atolls or uninhabited rocks stranded in the middle of the sea, and each one is utterly different. Some islands have long white talcum powder beaches, they have palm trees, they have turquoise seas, and they have beach bars with friendly waiters pouring endless pitchers of potent pina coladas.

Then, on the other hand, there are other islands with lush green mountains and steep valleys stippled with brilliant tropical flowers where rare parrots scream overhead and tiny lizards scuttle underfoot. These are for the more energetic and inquisitive nature-lovers.

There are French islands with seaside restaurants for gourmets; there are British islands with ruined forts for historians; there are American islands with fast catamarans and so slow tropical coral reefs; and there are islands where a whole kaleidoscope of races, African, Indian, European, South American, come together for the biggest, noisiest, wildest party of the year, where the visitor can dress up and dance until dawn and still have the energy to do it all again tomorrow. There is something here for everyone. What's your poison?

Market day on Dominica. This is a climate where almost anything will grow

THOMAS COOK'S
Caribbean

Interest in the Caribbean as a holiday destination grew during World War I when Thomas Cook, unable to provide Americans with their favourite holidays in Europe, began to encourage them to visit the Caribbean. Ten years later the region became popular as a cruise destination when the company advertised sailings from New York to St Thomas, St Croix, St Kitts, Antigua, Guadeloupe, Dominica, Martinique and St Lucia. But the Caribbean's popularity was finally sealed after World War II when air travel brought the warmth of the islands even closer.

History

1000BC
The Ciboney people are thought to be the first Amerindians to settle.
AD200
The Arawaks follow.
800
The warlike Caribs cross the region.
1493
Columbus' second voyage takes him to Dominica and Guadeloupe.
1498
Columbus' third voyage takes him to Trinidad and St Vincent.
1499
Juan de la Cosa spies St Lucia.
1536
The Portuguese explorer Pedro a Campos lands on Barbados.
1623
British and French settle on St Kitts.
1627
British colonists settle on Barbados.
1635
The French occupy Martinique.
1648
France and Holland divide up St Martin/St Maarten.
1671
Danish settle on St Thomas.
1782
French capture all British islands except Barbados and Antigua.
1782
The Battle of the Saintes.
1783
Peace treaty between Britain and France leads to British dominance on the islands.
1784
The French hand St Barthélemy to Sweden in exchange for trade rights.
1797
Britain takes Trinidad from the Spanish.
1814–15
The Treaties of Paris allot Martinique and Guadeloupe to France and most of the other islands to Britain.
1834
The British parliament abolishes slavery.
1848
The French abolish slavery on their islands.
1863
The Dutch outlaw slavery on the Netherlands' Antilles.
1878
St Barthélemy reverts to France.
1958
The West Indies Federation is formed.
1962
Trinidad and Tobago become a presidential republic within the British Commonwealth.
1966
Barbados achieves independence.
1967
Antigua, St Kitts and Nevis, Anguilla, St Lucia, St Vincent and Dominica become Associated States within the Commonwealth.
1974
Grenada achieves independence.
1978
Dominica becomes an independent republic.
1979
St Lucia and St Vincent and the Grenadines achieve independence.
1981
Antigua and Barbuda become independent.
1983
St Kitts and Nevis win independence. The United States invades Grenada to restore political stability.

Geography

*T*he islands featured in this book, known as the Lesser Antilles, comprise a 1,500km border between the Caribbean Sea and the Atlantic Ocean, curving southwards from the Virgin Islands to Trinidad and Tobago. On one side the Atlantic pounds against rocky coasts covered with scrubby vegetation; on the other the much gentler Caribbean Sea laps against long sandy beaches.

Most of the islands in the northern part of the chain form a group which has historically been known as the Leeward Islands; those to the south of them have been termed the Windward Islands; Trinidad and Tobago are part of what used to be known as the southern Caribbean.

Geology

Geologically, the majority of these islands are volcanic and evidence of volcanic activity can be seen in some of the region's most striking landmarks, such as the Pitons on St Lucia and the Quill on St Eustatius. While there is no longer much volcanic action, there are still steam-filled gorges and boiling pools of mud on Martinique, Guadeloupe, Dominica and St Vincent. Those islands not of volcanic origin are mostly small, low-lying coral atolls with barrier reefs and sandy beaches. Most of the sea around the islands is on the continental shelf and relatively shallow.

Flora

Although the flora of the region ranges from succulents and scrub to lush green rainforest, the Caribbean is particularly famous for its tropical flowers and trees. Coconut palms are everywhere, of course, but they pale in comparison with something like a flametree in full bloom. Many of the flowers – hibiscus, bougainvillaea, frangipani – are so commonplace to the region they have somehow been relegated to a lower league; however, there are also hundreds of rarer and more exotic species.

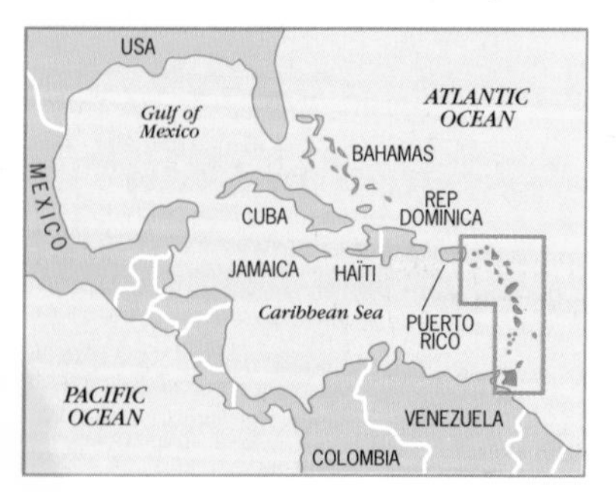

THE PEOPLE BEFORE COLUMBUS

Although arguments continue unabated among academics, popular mythology contends there were two principal races of Amerindians in the eastern Caribbean before the Europeans arrived. The Arawaks, who came first, are said to have been a peaceful tribe, living in small communities by the sea, eating whatever food they could catch and growing a few crops such as maize and cassava. By contrast, the Caribs are reputed to have been a fierce, warlike people who fought the incoming colonists in a series of bloody battles, ultimately choosing suicide rather than capture.

EASTERN CARIBBEAN

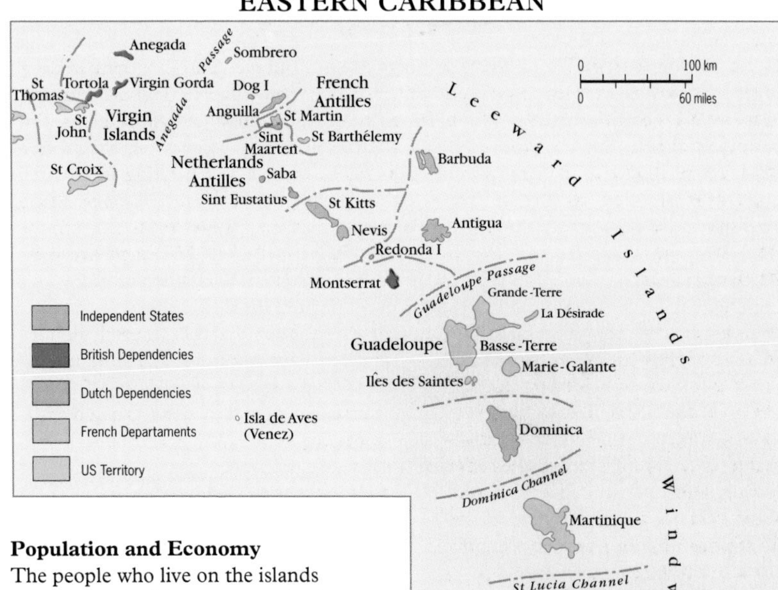

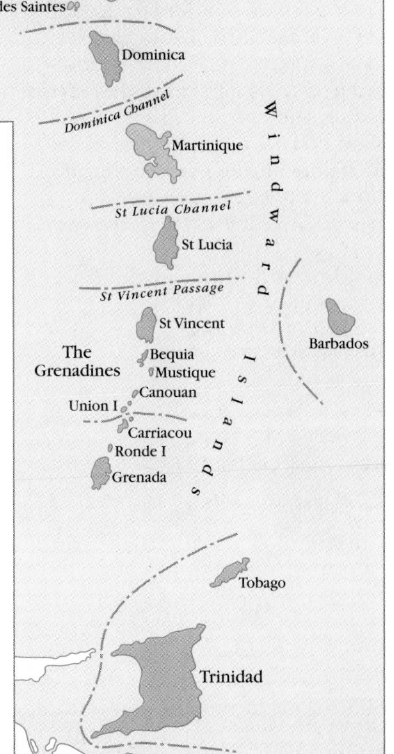

Population and Economy

The people who live on the islands around the Caribbean are mostly the descendants of African slaves shipped across the Atlantic to work on the plantations in the 17th and 18th centuries. A few islanders, however, can trace their family trees directly to the Caribs who came from South America before the first Europeans. The rest of the population are either descendants of the colonial settlers or of the indentured workers from East India who arrived when slavery was abolished, or else they are more recent arrivals, attracted by the climate or various business opportunities.

Virtually all the islands rely heavily on tourism to keep their economies afloat. There is still a considerable amount of farming on the Lesser Antilles but, while sugar is still important on islands such as Guadeloupe and St Kitts, it is not as vital to the region as it once was. There is also some light industry.

Culture

The distinctive culture of any Caribbean island today – the way the majority of people eat, sleep, talk, dance and sing, the way they live their lives together in their own communities – has been influenced by many different groups of people in that island's history. This is a mixture of ingredients which is often referred to as if it had been added to some all-embracing melting pot which had then blended it into a homogenous broth; but some flavours come through more powerfully than others.

There is a strong movement in the Caribbean region now to recognise the value of the most important historical influences, and to preserve them in their oldest existing forms as long as possible.

Caribbean people are no longer content with the old colonial view of history: these islands were not discovered by Columbus, they say, people were already living on them by then. Indeed, studies have shown that Arawak and Carib words still exist in island vocabularies. Modern interpretations of Amerindian handicrafts are proudly promoted in the tourist shops.

Oral history and folk research projects have emphasised the importance of the slave culture to modern island life. The slaves were the largest group of people to come to the islands and the African element is considered by many to be the strongest flavour in the Caribbean's cultural mix. The structure of village society, for example, is traced back to West Africa, the architecture of many of the houses betrays African roots, and the knowledge of bush medicine, which still exists today, came

Sunday best on St Kitts

NICKNAMES

Everyone has a nickname in the Caribbean. If they are tall, they may be called Shorty; if they own a noisy car they might be called Toot-toot. Sometimes there is a less obvious reason for the nickname; occasionally it is a *jumbie* (ghost) name given to appease a dead person or to honour a deceased relative. No one, not even the socially disadvantaged, is excluded. A man with one foot might be called Hop Scotch; an ugly boy might be called Handsome. It is one of the ways Caribbean society accepts and accommodates all its members, leaving no one feeling left out.

Steel drums and painted dancers – elements of lifestyle on Antigua

across with the slave ships.

To celebrate this African legacy, traditional foods are prepared at festivals, the modern derivatives of old musical instruments are played at staged events, folk dances are studied and performed in the old style again, and story tellers, or raconteurs, rework traditional folk tales at special celebrations. Even the language of the people has changed its status from a poor uneducated pidgin tongue to a language which deserves to be studied in its own right.

SUPERSTITIONS

Many of the old superstitions still exist in the Caribbean today; fishermen on Tobago believe that spraying their boats with oils and ointments brings good luck, and that whistling at sea scares the fish away; farmers, on the other hand, will not plant crops when there has been a funeral in the village, and believe they should bathe themselves before entering their plot of yams.

The silk cotton tree found on several islands is wrapped up in the African belief in life after death and reminds those still alive they should not forget the ways, customs and traditions of their African ancestors who have gone to *jumbie* (ghost) country. In Montserrat, *jumbie* dances are based on an African tribal ritual and lead to a trance-like state, ostensibly bringing together the world of the living and the world of the dead for the good of the living, while in Dominica, a few people still take baths of special herbs and cast spells on the heads of their enemies.

Politics

Given the number of different governments and administrations in the eastern Caribbean, the region is remarkably stable and visitors have little to fear from political unrest. Only the events in Grenada in 1983, when the short-lived People's Revolution got out of hand, and in Port of Spain in 1990, when a group of Muslims took over Parliament, have disturbed the equilibrium in recent years. Yet this is politically one of the most fragmented areas in the world, thanks initially to the colonial carve-up of the region and latterly to the islands' own strong sense of identity.

Several islands in the chain still nestle in the bosom of European powers. The islands of Martinique and Guadeloupe, for example, are overseas *départements* of France; Montserrat and the British Virgin Islands are British Crown Colonies; the Netherlands Antilles – St Maarten, Saba and St Eustatius – remain within the Kingdom of the Netherlands; the US Virgin Islands is a territory of the United States. Others are more loosely associated with their former colonial owners. St Lucia, Barbados and Antigua are all independent members of the British Commonwealth; while Trinidad and Tobago form a parliamentary republic also within the Commonwealth.

The Union Jack still flies over some islands

Attempts have been made, over the last 40 years, to knit the islands more closely together for the common good. The West Indies Federation, formed in 1958 and incorporating former British colonies, fell apart four years later. Then, in 1968, the Caribbean Free Trade Area was founded, to be succeeded, in 1973, by Caricom, the Caribbean Common Market.

However, this has proved a loose association and many people feel that if the Caribbean region is to have an effective voice in the modern world and is to promote effectively export businesses in the face of challenges from emerging nations, the islands will have to bind themselves much more closely together, politically and economically, in years to come.

FIRST STEPS

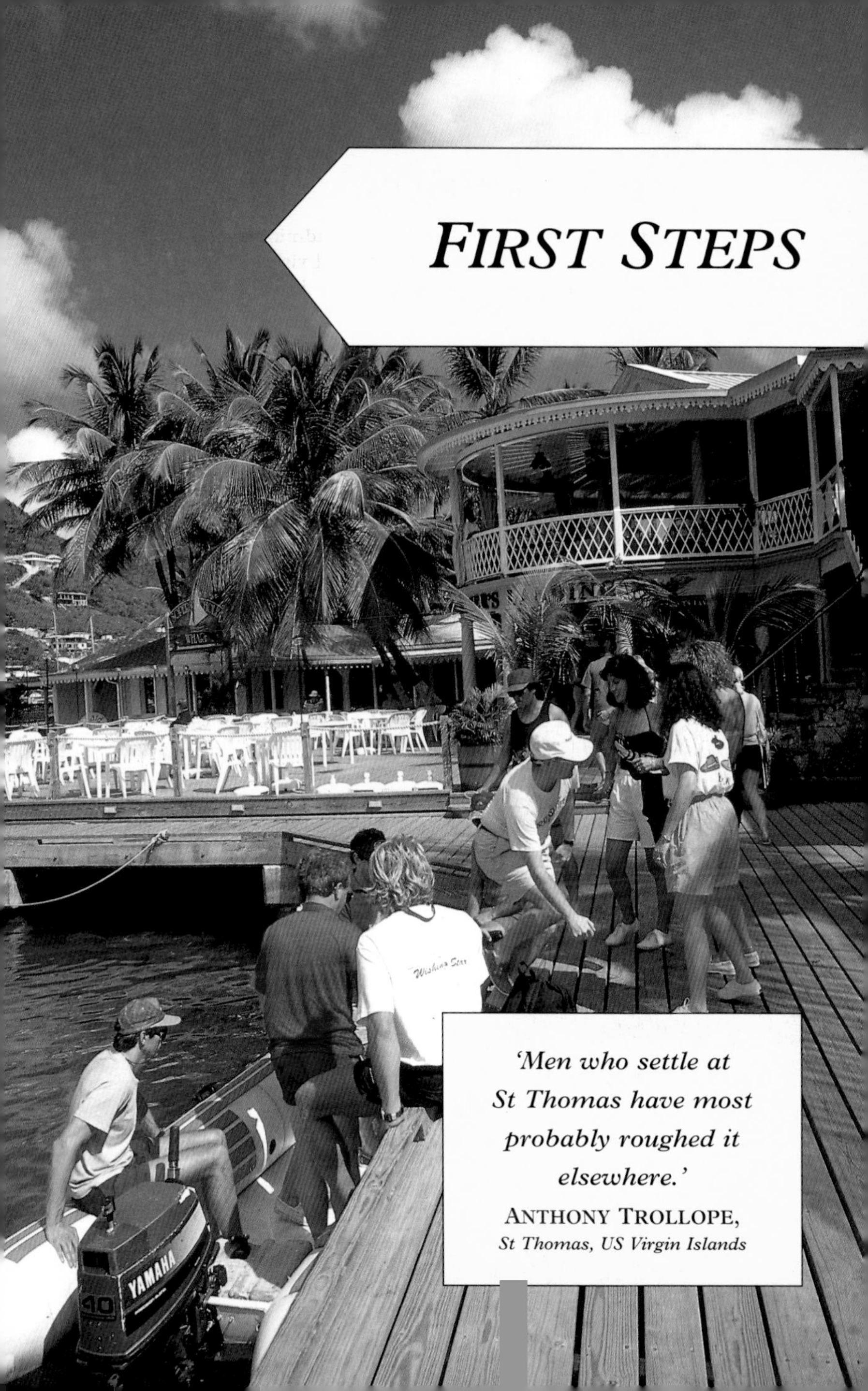

'Men who settle at St Thomas have most probably roughed it elsewhere.'

ANTHONY TROLLOPE,
St Thomas, US Virgin Islands

Nearly all islanders are friendly and will respond to your openness

It may seem a simple business, flying off to the sun and relaxing in the tropics for a week or two, but there is an art to getting the best out of a Caribbean trip from the moment you leave the aeroplane, to the final farewell.

CULTURE SHOCK

They are everywhere; milling around airports in a daze, hanging around hotel lobbies looking drained, peering at the pool with tired blood-shot eyes, a briefcase in one hand, a welcome cocktail wrapped in a soggy napkin in the other.

The new arrivals are not hard to spot. They invariably look pallid and grey from some intemperate northern climate; their clothes are crumpled from hours squashed into a 747; they are hot, they are bothered – and they are ready to pick a fight the moment anyone tells them their room is not ready yet or their luggage will be here in ten minutes. They are so stressed they are ready to explode.

It does not have to be like that. The key to setting off on the right foot is to begin the holiday while still sitting on the aeroplane, to decide that nothing is going to be an irritant, to relax into a state of serenity that will last until the end of the holiday.

There will be times when the island telephone system, or the speed of service in the restaurant, or the local inter-island airline will bring the visitor to screaming point (to the point when going on holiday seems like harder work than staying at home and going to the office); but that practised state of calm, that imperturbable cheerfulness will save the day and everybody's nerves. It is a Caribbean cliché – 'Don't worry, be happy' – but it is a motto best worn on both sleeves.

SAY HELLO

There is nothing Caribbean islanders like less or distrust more than a surly po-faced tourist and there is no place here for ice-cool northern reserve. The Caribbean has a history of superior white folk bossing the blacks around and has no intention of going back to that sorry state.

It is easy to make friends and to get along with people on the islands; all it takes is a cheery greeting and an open-handed, friendly approach. In smaller villages this may well mean saying hello to everybody in the street; there is no harm in that and it gives tourists a good name. Staff in island hotels certainly respond to an affable approach; many of them wear name badges and the effort of remembering and using the name of the waiter or the chambermaid as soon as possible is often rewarded with some useful inside island knowledge and advice.

It is absolutely essential to ask permission before taking a photograph of anyone. Islanders take great exception to having a camera pointed in their direction as if they were exhibits at the zoo; if you find this difficult to understand, imagine how you would feel.

Clichés are usually true: in the Caribbean people really are laid back

Stay cool, and smile at the world

SUNBURN

More holidays are ruined by sunburn than by anything else. It seems nannyish to say so, but it is wise to spend no more than 15–20 minutes exposed to the sun in the middle of the day, at least until a base tan has had a chance to establish itself. Always use a high-factor sunscreen when out and about, even when the sky seems cloudy. Hats can be bought at a local market, and good sunglasses are necessary to protect the eyes from the midday glare.

GETTING AROUND

There are several ways of exploring the islands; by private transport or by public transport, by land or by sea. Caribbean taxi drivers are a more cheerful breed, on the whole, than many of their counterparts around the world, and for a fee – often quite a sizeable fee, but one which can occasionally be negotiated downwards – they will, almost without exception, be willing and able to conduct a guided tour of the main tourist sights on the island. This is a good way to see the place for the first day or two, but after that it can be more fun to explore independently. Hotels and tourist offices have a list of car hire firms; occasionally, on small islands, these companies also supply scooters and bicycles. As an alternative to the often sterile world of the private car, however, many people enjoy the experience of taking public transport, affording as it does an opportunity to meet or at least to mingle with the islanders as they go about their daily lives. Nearly every island has some inexpensive way of getting from A to B. More often than not this is a minibus, known variously as a taxi, a bus, a taxi collectif or a maxi-taxi, and it usually advertises its destination or route on the front (if in doubt check with the driver).

All of the islands are linked by regular plane flights. Some airlines offer special tickets which enable extended travel at limited cost

Mini moke is an ideal form of transport for touring the islands

At rush hours these minibuses are often crammed to capacity and occasionally every single passenger may have to climb out to let some poor soul at the back alight at his stop; but that seldom seems to bother anybody. It is also common for passengers to pass the bus fare from hand to hand up the bus until it reaches the driver or his assistant.

But be warned; these taxis or minibuses often double as mobile discos. It seems you judge a Caribbean driver not by the company he keeps but by the quality and volume of his in-car stereo and his choice of music. It is unwise to ask him to turn it down.

Other forms of transport take the tourist right away off any beaten track. On smaller islands, for example, local water taxis can be hired to hug the coast to some deserted beach or rocky cove. A price should be agreed beforehand and a firm arrangement for the return journey sorted out. Tours through the countryside on foot or on horseback can sometimes be arranged, offering a fascinating glimpse of the island that few other visitors see.

Virgin Islands ferry

ISLAND HOPPING

Having travelled maybe several thousand kilometres to holiday in the Caribbean, it would be a pity to see just one island. All the islands are connected by boat or aeroplane, and local tourist offices and airlines will supply timetables and a list of connections. Some of the best journeys are the shortest: the 21m schooner with the mail from Grenada to Carriacou, for instance, the ferry from St Vincent to Bequia, or the flight from St Maarten/St Martin into Saba.

However, island-hopping involves careful planning and it is advisable to include a degree of flexibility within those plans. Inter-island flights and ferries, like any public transport service, are subject to occasional cancellations, bad weather and excessive demand. It pays to re-confirm bookings frequently and to ensure arrangements at the other end have some slack built into them. And it is always wise to make sure that a short trip away returns to the base island at least two days before the final departure date.

DAILY ROUTINE

It often comes as a relief to the perspiring visitor to find that even the people who have been living on the islands all their lives sometimes find it hot. Despite the proliferation of ice-cold air-conditioning systems in banks, hotels, offices and shops, the daily grind still starts early in the islands when the air is cool, before the shadows harden; and most physical activities, sports and games, take place in the dying heat of the late afternoon and early evening. Although there is officially no such thing as a siesta in the Caribbean, villages are often at their quietest in the middle of the day and shops are frequently closed then; if they have time, people sit on their verandas or 'lime-out', as the saying goes, in chairs and hammocks.

WHAT TO SEE

'Port of Spain. What a legendary and romantic town the syllables evoke!'

PATRICK LEIGH FERMOR,
Trinidad

US Virgin Islands

*T*he motto on the car licence plates reads 'American Paradise' and that is a view shared by many of the 2 million or so tourists who arrive on these shores every year. Most of them carry US driver licences – and large shopping bags, for these islands, particularly St Thomas, are considered to offer the best duty-free shopping in the Caribbean.

Of the 50 or so islands, islets and little cays which make up the US Virgins (pop. 105,000), only three are permanently inhabited: St Thomas, St John and St Croix, which together form a territory of the United States with their own locally elected resident governor.

VIRGIN ISLANDS

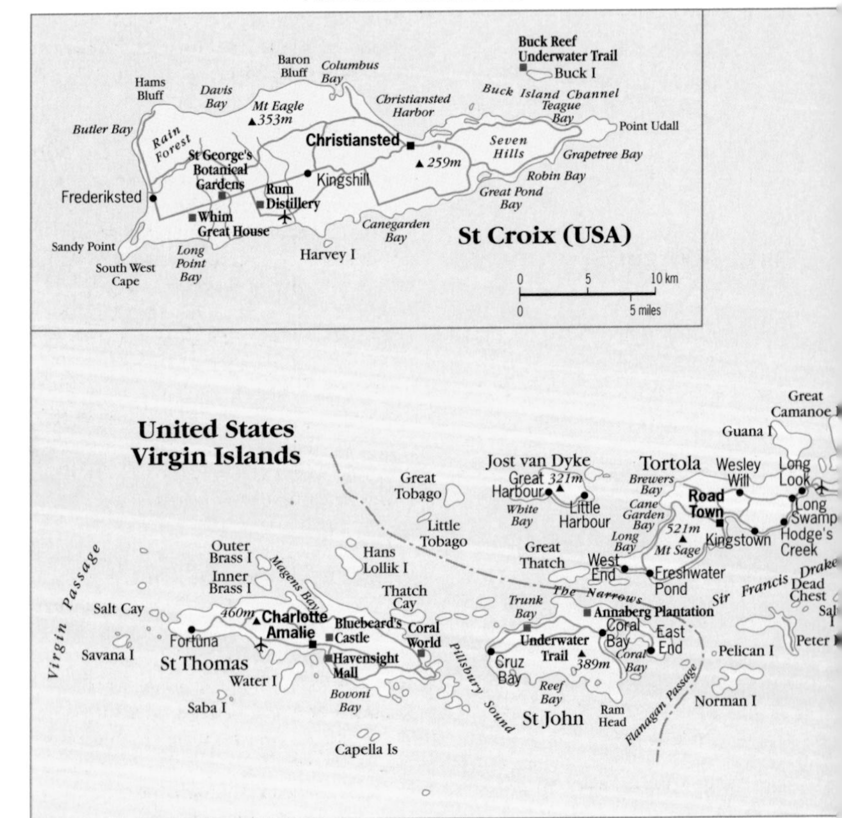

Columbus first sighted the islands on his second voyage in 1493. Arriving at an island known to the native Carib Indians as Ayay and rechristening it Santa Cruz (St Croix), he claimed the islands in the name of Spain. But Spain actually had little interest in them and ultimately it was the Danish Government which declared the islands a Crown colony. On 31 March 1917, the United States, concerned about protecting the Panama Canal, bought the islands from Denmark for $25 million.

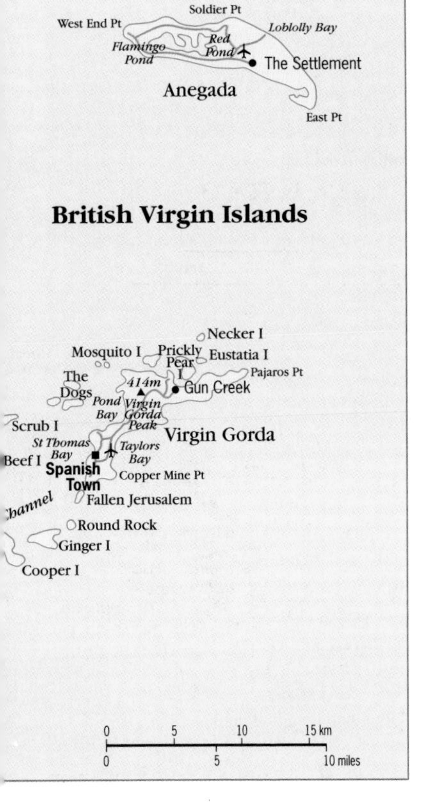

ST THOMAS

Thousands of cruise ship passengers invade St Thomas every day, most of them with just one thing on their mind – shopping. The more adventurous visitor, however, soon discovers that there is more to St Thomas than bargains.

CHARLOTTE AMALIE

Charlotte Amalie is a picturesque place – a tumble of pantiled, whitewashed houses gathered round a deep horseshoe bay. For all its commercial glitz, a sense of history still pervades the town. The centre of town is listed in the US National Register of Historic Places. (See also page 24.)

CORAL WORLD

This 2-hectare marine park at Coki Point features one of the few underwater observation towers in the western hemisphere, providing the non-swimmer with a chance to come face to face with an ever-changing procession of sealife.
Coki Point Beach (tel: 775 1555). Open: daily, 9am–6pm. Admission charge.

DRAKE'S SEAT

According to legend, Sir Francis Drake used to sit at this point on Skyline Drive watching Spanish galleons in the strait.
Skyline Drive above Magens Bay.

MAGENS BAY

This kilometre-long crescent of sand features in several lists of the world's best beaches. There is also an educational trail which leads through areas of archaeological interest as well as of natural beauty. Details of a short self-guided tour are available from the kiosk at the entrance to the bay or from the Virgin Islands Planning Office.
Magens Road. Admission charge.

Much of St John is a nature reserve and covered in jungle

ST JOHN

Only a short 20-minute ferry ride from St Thomas, St John could hardly be more different. No less than two thirds of this island consists of national park and although there are a handful of boutiques around Cruz Bay, most people come to get closer to nature. Some take an island tour on the safari-style, open-sided taxi-buses which line up by the dock; others just head straight for one of the island's beautiful beaches.

ANNABERG PLANTATION

This is one of the best-preserved 18th-century sugar plantations in the region. It was first referred to on a map of 1780 as one of 25 active sugar-producing estates on the island. In addition to the familiar windmill, you find the remains of the circular horse-drawn mill, the slave quarters and the cane sugar boiling bench. Several days a week local residents explain how the plantation worked. Check with the Park Service for details.

Near Leinster Bay. Admission free.

PARK SERVICE VISITOR CENTRE

The first port of call for many tourists is just a short walk from the ferry jetty. Here you learn about the flora and fauna of the island, there are cultural demonstrations, wildlife lectures and evening programmes, and you can also pick up a guide to the various hiking trails which criss-cross the island.

Cruz Bay (tel: 776 6201). Open: Monday to Friday, 8am–5pm. Admission free.

ST CROIX

Although St Thomas is the administrative centre of the US Virgin Islands, St Croix, 65km further south, is actually bigger. Somehow it manages to strike a balance between the rampant commercialism of St Thomas and the peaceful tranquillity of St John. It also retains the stronger sense of its Danish history.

CHRISTIANSTED

The larger of St Croix's two towns, Christiansted was made the Danish colonial capital in 1734. Fortunately a discriminatory building code which came into effect a few years later preserved many of the original buildings for posterity.

Close to the King's Wharf, Fort Christiansvaern, rebuilt in 1837, is the best preserved Danish fort in the US Virgin Islands.

Fort Christiansvaern. Open: weekdays, 8am–5pm; weekends, 9am–5pm. Admission charge.

FREDERIKSTED

Frederiksted is a remarkably pretty, sleepy old town of colonial buildings, a great many of which are constructed in the Victorian 'gingerbread' style. The most interesting buildings, even better preserved than Christiansted, are in the grid of streets between Fort Frederick and the Customs House.

ST GEORGE'S BOTANICAL GARDENS

In the grounds of what was once an Arawak Indian village, 6·5 hectares of tropical gardens are landscaped around the ruins of a sugar plantation. Some 800 species of trees and plants can be seen by following the trails through rainforest, ruined estate buildings, an old rum factory, and a tropical orchard.

6·4km east of Frederiksted. Open: daily, 7.30am–3.30pm. Admission charge.

Promenading in Christiansted, where many Danish colonial buildings remain

WHIM GREAT HOUSE

The sugar era left a distinct mark on St Croix, a legacy of broken-down windmills and estate-owners' houses (greathouses). The Whim Plantation Museum includes one of the best preserved of these greathouses, the grand homes of the plantation owners. Here, visitors are taken on a lively tour that describes the life of one of the island's best-known sugar families, while outside they are free to explore the restored plantation buildings.

32km off Centerline Road near Frederiksted (tel: 772 0598). Open: Tuesday to Saturday, 10am–3pm. Admission charge.

SNORKELLING TRAILS

For an easy introduction to snorkelling, try one of the two trails laid out by the US National Parks Service. One is at the very popular Trunk Bay on St John, the other at Buck Reef on St Croix. A sign beside the beach marks the point of entry into the water, then a series of blue underwater plaques directs swimmers along a short undersea trail and describes some of the sights along the way.

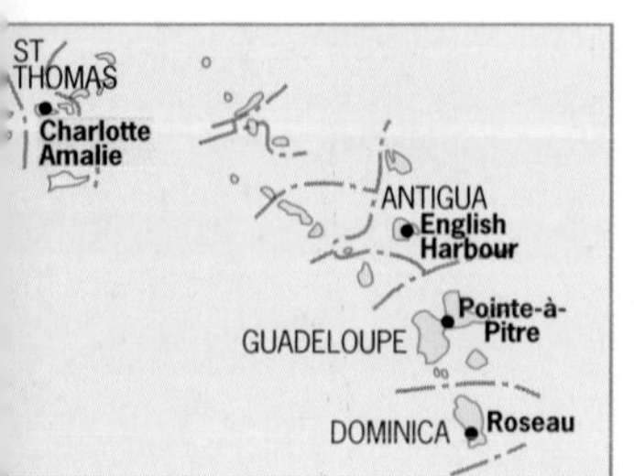

Around Charlotte Amalie (St Thomas)

This tour explores some of the historical highlights of Charlotte Amalie. Avoid the middle (hottest) part of the day. There is no admission charge to any of the sights. All the buildings will be open if you start the tour on a weekday at 9am. *Allow 2 hours.*

Start outside the two-storey pale green building on the waterfront beside Fort Christian.

1 LEGISLATURE OF THE VIRGIN ISLANDS

This arcaded building of 1874 was used initially as a barracks for Danish Police. Now it is the seat of the Legislature of the Virgin Islands. Enter by the centre door downstairs and climb the stairs to view the senate chambers.

Leave by the outside staircase and – remembering the traffic drives on the left – cross the road to Fort Christian.

2 FORT CHRISTIAN

The oldest structure still in use in the territory, until recently the island jail. Now officially declared a National Historic Sight, it houses an exhibit of life on St Thomas from earliest

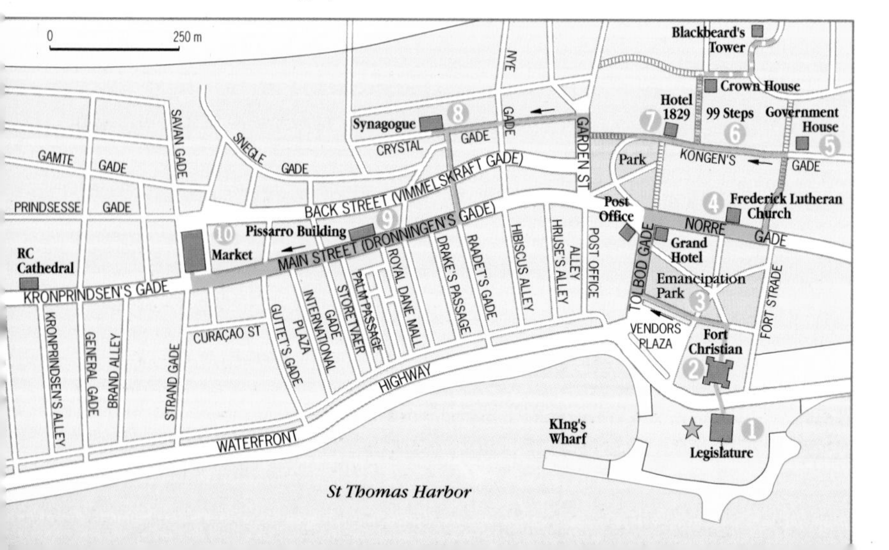

times, as well as examples of the island's wildlife.

Leaving the fort, walk down to your left.

3 EMANCIPATION PARK

This open space commemorates the freeing of the slaves by Governor Peter von Scholten on 3 July 1848.

A short stroll up Tolbod Gade takes you to Norre Gade. Turn right.

4 FREDERICK LUTHERAN CHURCH

An early 19th-century structure built in the Gothic Revival style, the Frederick Lutheran Church occupies the site of two earlier churches. Look in particular at the antique chandeliers and the plaques dedicated to early Danish settlers.

Take the first turning on the left and a short walk uphill to reach Kongen's Gade.

5 GOVERNMENT HOUSE

This is the official residence of the Governor of the US Virgin Islands. Designed by four members of the Danish Colonial Council, none of them architects, it was completed in 1867.

6 THE 99 STEPS

Although there are actually 103 stone steps leading up Government Hill, these have always been known as The 99 Steps. The bricks used to make them originally travelled from Denmark as ballast in the holds of sailing ships. An optional detour takes you up the steps to Blackbeard's castle and the remains of Fort Skytsborg (now an hotel and restaurant with stunning views).

Continue walking along Kongen's Gade.

7 HOTEL 1829

One of the best hotels on the island, Hotel 1829 was originally known as Lavalette House and was built for a French sea captain.

There are some steep steps leading down to Garden Street. Here you turn right, then left into Crystal Gade where there is a steep climb to the synagogue.

8 THE SYNAGOGUE OF BERECHA V'SHALOM V'GEMILATH CHASIDIM

This is the second oldest synagogue in the western hemisphere. Note the mahogany ark containing the holy scrolls on the right and the sand-covered floor. Legend suggests this symbolises the flight of the Jewish people across the desert; another explanation is that it is a legacy from the time the Jewish religion was practised in considerable secrecy and sand was used to muffle the sounds of prayer.

Return down Crystal Gade as far as Raadet's Gade and then walk down to Main Street (Dronningen's Gade) and turn right.

9 THE CAMILLE PISSARRO BUILDING

This was the birthplace and childhood home of the famous impressionist Camille Pissarro (1830–1903). In the passageway there is a description of the artist's early life on St Thomas.

A short walk further along Main Street leads to Rothschild Francis Market Square.

10 MARKET SQUARE

Once the site of one of the busiest slave markets in the Caribbean, the square is now the town's fruit and vegetable market; the old auction blocks have been covered with a wrought-iron roof.

The route back to the start of this walk – either by Main Street or along the waterfront – passes several old warehouses used in the days of slavery and pirates.

British Virgin Islands

An archipelago of over 50 islands, separated from their US sisters by little more than a line of dots on the map, the British Virgin Islands (pop. 16,750) look from the air like a group of squashed furry animals with scrubby backbones, paws splayed out towards the beaches and, in between, little white tics criss-crossing, changing hosts. This is the sailing capital of the world, and the tics are seriously expensive yachts. Island-hopping is the game here and if you do not have access to sails or a motor boat you use the inter island ferries.

TORTOLA

The largest island in the group, Tortola has a mountainous spine, with steep twisting roads and soft white beaches on its northern coast. The capital, Road Town, is a largely uninspiring town of commercial buildings, although the Main Street area behind Pusser's Store is very pleasant.

CALLWOOD RUM DISTILLERY

At the turn of the century more than 100 rum distilleries existed on Tortola. The Callwood Distillery is the last one to remain in use and the rum it produces is still made from sugar cane grown on the property, using exactly the same process as 150 years ago.

Cane Garden Bay. Open: Monday to Saturday (dependent on whether the distillery is working at the time).

Crowded waters around the islands

J R O'NEAL BOTANIC GARDENS

A cool and pleasant retreat close to the centre of Road Town, the Joseph Reynold O'Neal Botanic Gardens were officially opened in 1986. They cover just under 1·6 hectares and include the remains of a government experimental agricultural station first established 100 years ago. Here can be found an orchid house, rare tropical plants, a pergola walk, a lily pond, a small aviary and a miniature rainforest. A leaflet available at the entrance provides a walk route through the gardens and describes some of the plants and trees on view.

Station Avenue, Road Town. Open: daily during daylight hours. Admission free; donations.

SAGE MOUNTAIN NATIONAL PARK

Here, at the highest point on Tortola, is evidence of the forests which used to cover much of the island's backbone. The BVI National Parks Trust has laid out three walking trails around the summit; the first through a mahogany plantation, the second past an old forest knitted together with giant elephant ear vines, the third round a small loop trail, called the Henry Adams Trail, where the oldest and best-preserved trees are to be found. Even if you decide not to walk, the view from the car park is quite spectacular.

Take Joe's Hill Road from Road Town, then leave the Ridge Road at the signs for Sage Mountain. Admission free.

THE VIRGIN ISLANDS FOLK MUSEUM

Situated in Road Town, this museum has artefacts from the time of the Arawak Indians, including a collection of stones depicting the Arawak gods Yuccahu and

A miscellany of flotsam and jetsam put to use on a Tortola beach bar

Julihu. There are also a number of items salvaged from the wreck of the British Royal Mail Steamer, *Rhone*, which sank off Salt Island in 1867. Near by, the Sunday Morning Well on Upper Main Street is believed to be where the Proclamation of Emancipation was made in 1834; a plaque on the side of the well commemorates the event.

Main Street, Road Town. Open: Monday, Tuesday, Thursday, Friday, 10am–4pm; Saturday 10am–1pm. Admission free.

ANEGADA

Totally different from the other islands in topography, Anegada ('the drowned land') is a coral atoll known for its circle of white-sand beaches. It is a low flat island, 32km to the northeast of Tortola, which gets its name because it seems as if there is little to stop the waves rolling right over the top of it. Once the lair of pirates, Anegada is ringed by treacherous reefs which have trapped more than 200 ships over the years, many of them still visible in the surf. It is very popular with snorkellers and divers.

A palm-shaded bar and safe anchorage on Jost Van Dyke

JOST VAN DYKE

Just 6·4km north of St John and a stone's throw from Tortola, Jost Van Dyke is named after a notorious Dutch pirate. It is a long narrow island, with hills like camels' humps running along its length, but it is particularly renowned for its safe anchorage and beautiful beaches which make it popular with visiting yachts. The main town is **Great Harbour**, a village of picturesque wooden houses on a sandy bay surrounded by hilly peaks; to the west, long **White Bay** is also popular.

SALT ISLAND

With a population of just two permanent residents, this was once a traditional source of salt for local islands and for passing ships, and visitors will find that salt is still harvested here today. Close by is the Wreck of The Rhone, one of the best-known dive sites in the Caribbean. The 95m Royal Mail steamer, *Rhone,* sank during a hurricane in 1867. Now the remains of the wreck, lying in 6–24m of water, have been made the centrepiece of an open-access **marine park** covering some 320 hectares.

VIRGIN GORDA

The best-known tourist attraction on Virgin Gorda, 8km east of Tortola, is a tumble of huge, pale-grey granite boulders south of Spring Bay that form a network of caves, grottoes and pools known simply as **The Baths**. Completely different from other rock formations in the area, they have puzzled geologists for many years although some experts say they resemble rocks found on the coast of the Carolinas and may have resulted from Ice Age convulsions. The area becomes extremely busy most days with visiting yachts and boatloads of cruise ship passengers, so the best time to visit is either early in the morning or in the late afternoon. Alternatively, to escape the crowds, take a short 15-minute walk from the Baths along a scenic trail to **Devil's Bay National Park**, a secluded coral sand beach.

The ruins of an 18th-century stone, coral-and-brick sugar mill can be seen at **Nail Bay**, while on the southwest tip of the island there are the remains of a **Copper Mine** (the chimney, boiler house, cistern and mine shafts) worked by Cornish miners between 1838 and 1867. **Gorda Peak**, a national park

Not beached whales, but rocks; The Baths, Virgin Gorda

climbing to the island's highest point, contains a wide variety of indigenous and exotic plants and has been replanted with mahogany trees.

The Baths are at the southwest of the island, the Copper Mine at the far southeast, Gorda Peak in the middle of the main land mass to the north. Admission free.

NORMAN ISLAND

Popular legend suggests Norman Island was the setting for Robert Louis Stevenson's book *Treasure Island* and that the treasure from the Nuestra Senora was recovered here in 1750. It is also remarkable for its four caves which can be reached by boat at **Treasure Point.** Near by, **The Indians** is a series of tall rock formations which are said to look like an Indian headdress, while **Fallen Jerusalem**, another national park, resembles the ruins of an ancient city when viewed from the sea.

PETER ISLAND

A short ferry ride across Sir Francis Drake Channel from Tortola, this island is almost entirely owned by one local fisherwoman. Here are to be found the Peter Island Hotel and yacht harbour, while the beach at **Deadman's Cay** is one of the best in the BVIs.

Other Virgin Islands include Cooper Island, Ghana Island, Sandy Cay and Necker Island.

VILLAGE LIFE

A strong community spirit still lives on in the islands' many villages. Although it may look no more than a dozen shacks, a shop and a little church, the village enjoys a feeling of togetherness, of common purpose. While many islanders may travel away from home to look for work in hotels or even in well-paid jobs overseas, they still return for important occasions or, if they cannot get back, send money to support their home village.

Tourism is a double-edged sword; while it has enticed many of the village's most able workers away, by the same token it has often brought jobs back into its very core. Old skills such as weaving and carving are rediscoverd in the making of handicrafts for sale in the islands' tourist shops, and old songs and stories are revived to entertain visitors.

In most things, there tends to be a pragmatic approach to what the villagers decide to take from the outside world. For example, while modern medicines may save the lives of people who might otherwise have died, some of the traditional old cures are still in use. Why go all the way to town for a proprietary medicine from the pharmacist when a hot infusion of wild sage leaves will sort out a cough and cold?

The outside world may not always be consulted, but it often inveigles its way into villagers' homes. The lure of

television and its side-kick, the video, for example, is irresistible and is perhaps the greatest threat to village life. The video diet available from island shops comes almost entirely out of Hollywood, while cable pictures are relayed direct from Miami or New York. Local stations are underfunded and community television is still in its infancy. Unless it comes soon – or if a better way is not found to involve the village in this television age – everyday village life will be reduced to watching pictures of the latest massacre in a hamburger bar in Detroit.

Scenes from the Caribbean day-to-day. The hats and bowls at far left are made from palm leaves

Anguilla

Anguilla (pop 10,500) is a British territory that has the remarkable distinction of having rebelled in order to remain a British territory. The problem arose in 1967 when Britain tried to persuade the island to become more permanently allied with St Kitts and Nevis. The Anguillans were more interested in severing their ties with the other two countries than cementing them and protested by burning down Government House. The British response was ultimately to invade the little island with a force of 300 paratroopers and eventually Anguilla was brought back into the fold. These days it is hard to imagine such drama here for, even if it is no longer the Caribbean's best-kept secret, Anguilla is still one of the most relaxing places to unwind in the whole of the Caribbean.

ANGUILLA'S BEACHES

There are more than 30 blinding white sandy beaches on Anguilla. The following are some of the best.

Captains Bay

One of the most secluded beaches on Anguilla; a small powder-white sandy cove. *Take the road northeast from Island Harbour; persevere to the end of the track.*

Anguilla's Road Bay

Little Bay

This is a perfect cameo of a sandy cove surrounded by sandstone cliffs and the snorkelling is good. There is little shade. *Take the dirt track from the old cottage hospital for 1km or so. Then walk down the steep winding path from the edge of the road.*

Rendezvous Bay

A superb 3km stretch of sand and a good place to watch the low-flying pelicans. *Take the road for Blowing Point then turn right towards Rendezvous Salt Pond.*

Road Bay, Sandy Ground

This bay is almost landlocked and very peaceful (jet-skis have been banned on the island). As this is where many yachts report to customs and immigration, it can get quite busy. It is also the main jumping-off point for Sandy Island. *Southwest of The Valley.*

Shoal Bay

This is the best-known and hence the

busiest, but with good reason. It tends to be quieter at the eastern end. The snorkelling is fabulous here; equipment may be hired at the main entrance to the beach, along with sun shades, towels, beach umbrellas and lockers.
In the north of the island.

THE FOUNTAIN
Arawak petroglyphs (rock-carvings) have been discovered around a pool area in a cave near Shoal Bay. At the time of writing the cave is closed to the public, but there are plans to open a museum here. Check with the local tourist office.

ISLAND HARBOUR
Many island paintings reflect the Anguillans' passion for the sea. At Island Harbour some of their distinctive brightly painted fishing boats can often be seen pulled up on the shore. These days, however, the old-style, traditional boats tend to be saved for racing. It is an island obsession and race day is one of the biggest events on the island calendar.

THE VALLEY
The administrative centre of the island is a sort of blink-and-you've-missed-it kind of place, although there are some pleasant art galleries and shops.

BIRDWATCHING ON ANGUILLA
Anguilla has a surprising amount of birdlife. There are colonies of frigates on Little Bay and Dog Island. One can spot herons, white-cheeked pintails and blue-winged teal on East End Pond and beautiful red-billed tropic birds make their nests in the cliffs above Little Bay. Ground doves can be seen throughout the island.

Rendezvous Bay. No Caribbean holiday is complete without 'coo' sunsets

NEVIS, ST KITTS, ST MARTIN, ANGUILLA

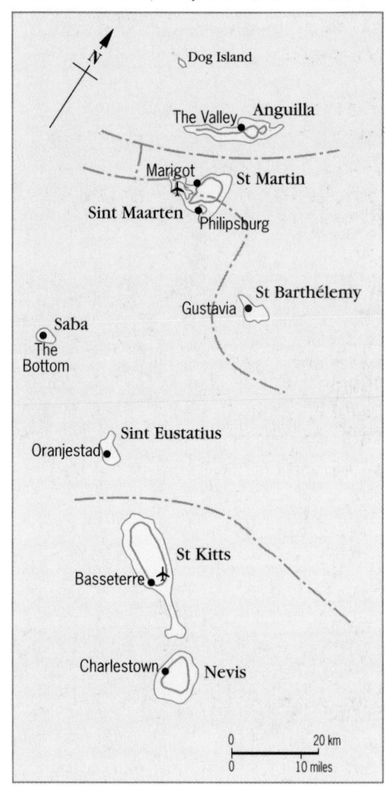

Sint Maarten/Saint Martin

St Maarten/St Martin has two names because this 96 sq km island actually boasts a dual nationality; it is half Dutch and half French. In the history of the Caribbean most islands have changed hands several times between colonial powers. In the case of St Maarten/St Martin, the Dutch and French forces decided to share the territory between them and, even more unusually, agreed to help each other out in times of need. Now only a sign at the side of the road indicates that you have crossed from France to Holland.

DUTCH SINT MAARTEN

PHILIPSBURG

This is the capital of Dutch St Maarten and the administrative centre of the three Dutch Windward Islands – St Maarten, Saba and St Eustatius – which, together with Bonaire and Curaçao, make up the Netherlands Antilles. Philipsburg was founded in 1733 as a freeport and this has been the source of its wealth ever since. Second only to Charlotte Amalie on the cruise ship circuit of duty free shopping opportunites, there is hardly a day when the paved Front Street is not thronged with bargain hunters weighed down with linen, crockery, cassette players and bottles of rum.

Philipsburg and its bays and beaches from the hills above

Fortunately there are some quieter havens away from the relentless world of commerce that is modern Philipsburg. **The Simartin Museum**, for example, on the first floor of a restored 19th-century house at the west end of Front Street, features books and artefacts relevant to the island's history (open: Monday to Friday, 10am–1pm. Admission free; donations). Immediately across the street is the 140-year-old **Philipsburg Methodist Church**, while beside the town square and close to the pier is the historic **Courthouse**, built in 1793 and twice renovated (not open). In its earliest history there was a weighing station on the ground floor, while the island's court sat on the upper floor and on important occasions the entire St Maarten Council would make an appearance on the balcony. At the east end of Front Street, the **West Indian Tavern** occupies a historic building dating from the late 18th century, once the home of a St Maarten governor and also, it is said, the former site of the island's synagogue.

Open space beneath Philipsburg's Courthouse

A walkway at the foot of Front Street leads over the hill to Little Bay and the ruins of Fort Amsterdam (open). Built in 1631, it was the first Dutch fort in the Caribbean. Two years later the Spanish captured it. After the Dutch Colonial governor Peter Stuyvesant tried to win the island back, the Spanish troops demolished much of the fort, finally leaving St Maarten to the Dutch and French in 1648. Until the 1950s it was a signalling and communications station.

ZOOLOGICAL AND BOTANICAL GARDEN

The theme of this 1·2 hectare garden, one of the island's newest attractions, is the plants and animals of the Caribbean basin and South America. There is also a substantial reptile collection.
Located directly across Great Salt Pond from Philipsburg. Open weekdays 9am–5pm; weekends and public holidays, 10am–6pm. Admission charge.

THE BORDER LINE
If the distribution of land between the French (52 sq km) and the Dutch (37sq km) seems less than fair, the islanders have a popular fable to explain why. A Frenchman and a Dutchman were chosen to walk round the island at the time the original treaty was signed. The border, it was decided, would be drawn wherever they eventually met. The reason France ended up with more territory than Holland, so the story goes, was all due to someone handing the Dutchman a bottle of gin as he was about to set off.

Quiet good taste combined with luxury accommodation on French St Martin

FRENCH SAINT MARTIN

MARIGOT

Tucked into the Baie de Marigot, the town of the same name is a quiet place compared to Philipsburg. Here there are proper pavements outside the shops and visitors can sit at a café and watch the world go by, as if they were in Paris or Nice, with a *café au lait* and *pain au chocolat.* Marigot is the capital of French St Martin although, technically, it is just the principal town of one *arrondissement* of Guadeloupe. But for all its French sophistication (and here you can buy clothes from the best fashion houses of France), it is still essentially a Caribbean town. Fishermen set off from its quay at dawn and a colourful fruit and vegetable market operates beside the T-shirt sellers.

The town has retained much of its historical and cultural tradition by conserving and restoring many of its gingerbread-decorated buildings. The best times to visit are on Saturday, Friday or Wednesday mornings when the market is at its busiest.

GRAND CASE

This is where many of the early settlers planted their sugar cane; now the Creole-style houses of the village are home to some of the island's best restaurants. It has gained a reputation for expensive *haute cuisine*, but it is also a good place to try authentic island specialities such as johnny cakes, plantains, peas and rice.
Location: in the north of French St Martin.

ST MAARTEN/ST MARTIN'S BEACHES

Baie de l'Embouchure

Also known as Coconut Grove, this is a sheltered bay protected by a reef just south of Orient Beach. The calm water is suitable for children and there are windsurfers for hire. Day sails and snorkelling excursions are also readily available.
Follow the signs for Orient Beach then turn left.

Cupecoy Beach

Next door to Long Bay, this is close to the site of one of the original Indian settlements on the island. It is a secluded stretch of sand, privacy provided by limestone cliffs which rise immediately behind the beach. Cars park on the corner of the road just before the French/Dutch border sign.

Dawn Beach

All of St Maarten/St Martin's beaches are public, so although access to Dawn Beach is through the Dawn Beach Hotel, anyone can sunbathe here. It gets its name from the particularly beautiful sunrises that can be seen from this part of the island.
Head east out of Philipsburg in the direction of Sucker Garden.

Grand Case Beach
The sea is usually calm here, so the swimming is good and the snorkelling at the south end is excellent.
Take the dirt track from Grand Case village in the north of the island.

Green Cay
Green Cay, a small island just off Orient Beach, is an good place to go snorkelling because of the calm clear waters surrounding its extensive coral formations.
Boat trips to the island can be arranged through the water sports operatives on Orient Beach.

Long Bay Beach
This beach seems to go on forever, beginning more or less at the western tip of Dutch St Maarten and stretching all the way to the Pointe du Canonnier. It is home to the famous La Samanna Hotel.
Take the road west of Philipsburg, passing the airport.

CLOTHING OPTIONAL
While most of the Caribbean prefers its tourists covered up, the French islands turn a blind eye to nudity. On St Martin, nude or topless sunbathing is common on the beaches. Orient Beach, the best-known strip of sand for stripping off, is the home of Club Orient, a very popular naturist holiday camp with about 80 Finnish-style log chalets close to the beach.

Plum Bay
Plum Bay is a continuation of Long Bay, on the western tip of the island. It is a beautiful white sandy beach but there is little natural shelter available.

Restaurant at Grand Case

St Barthélemy

St Barthélemy (pop. 3,500), or St Barts as it is better known, is almost indecently pretty. The smallest of the French West Indies – a mere 13 sq km of miniature hills, valleys, villages and beautiful white sand beaches – the island became a fashionable retreat 20 years ago for the rich and famous, a sort of Caribbean St Tropez in the tropics for Rothschilds and Rockefellers. While St Barts still attracts the moneyed set from around the world, a booming tourist economy also adds to the island's coffers.

Although the Amerindians knew it as Ouanalao, Christopher Columbus named the island after his brother, Bartolomeo. It was not until 1648 that the island was settled by Europeans when the first French colonists arrived from nearby St Kitts. In 1784, France sold St Barthélemy to Sweden in exchange for trading rights in the Baltic. The Swedes renamed the main port Gustavia after their king and declared the island a freeport, which it remained even after the French bought it back in 1878.

GUSTAVIA

A picturesque port of whitewashed, red-roofed houses, Gustavia successfully combines the contemporary tourist demands of a Caribbean town – a little history and a lot of shopping. Early French and Swedish buildings now house some of France's most exclusive names from the world of fashion, with

Street on St Barthélemy

prices to match. Some well-heeled visitors dive in; others seem content to shop or to sit under the trees in the courtyard of Le Select Bar, a social hub in the centre of town.

Fort Oscar, located at the tip of the peninsula, is in the best state of repair and still serves as home to the Ministry of Armed Forces; this unfortunately means visitors get no further than the front door. It is worth the struggle through the undergrowth to what is left of **Fort Karl**, overlooking the junior school, for its views across Gustavia and Grand-Galet. **Fort Gustave**, a 45m climb from the port, has recently been restored and visitors can tour the building, the old powder magazine and the kitchens. A panoramic plaque has been set up near by pointing out the neighbouring islands. None of these forts have opening times for the public; two, however, are accessible ruins.

Municipal Museum of Saint Barthélemy

This small museum has artefacts from the island's earliest history as well as more recent photographs of life on St Barts, and local island crafts.
On the west side of Gustavia harbour (tel: 27.89.07). Open: Monday to Thursday, 8am–noon and 1.30pm–5.30pm; Friday, 8am–noon and 1.30pm–5pm, Saturday, 8.30am–noon. Admission free.

COROSSOL

The fishing village of Corossol, about 2·5km north of Oustaria, is as close to provincial France as you can come in the Caribbean. The women, often dressed in traditional shoulder-length bonnets called *quichenottes,* sit outside their houses weaving baskets and hats. The men spend most of their time fishing at sea. Although it may seem a good place to practise tourist French, the people here in fact speak their own version of an old Norman dialect.

Gustavia Harbour

Inter-Oceans Museum

This curiosity is one of only two shell museums in the world. The curator will help to identify any unusual shells found on the beach.
Corossol (tel: 27 62 97). Open: daily, 10am–5pm. Admission charge.

SHELL COLLECTING

There are two reasons why St Barts is the ideal island for shell-collectors: Anse de Galet, a beach made up entirely of shells, and the Inter-Oceans Museum. Always make sure empty shells are collected; live shells should be returned to the sea. And take only one or two – there is little attraction in a shell beach without shells.

ISLAND STYLE

Colourful cottages, simple stone churches, colonial government buildings, imposing plantation greathouses; the history of the Caribbean is told as much in its buildings as in the faces of its people. There are styles of architecture derived from every period in each island's past, and a tour in the countryside or a walk round town will reveal much more about the people living there than a day on the beach.

For the most part, the buildings are of coral stone or brick brought in ships as ballast from foreign countries, and were built for the conditions, perhaps with wide windows to let in a cooling breeze or with thick walls to protect against hurricanes. It is usually the extra little details, however, that attract the eye, – the decorative fretwork, the intricate gingerbread, the moulding on the doors.

Sometimes it is simply a combination of colours which makes even the most primitive-looking houses attractive, whether on St Barthélemy, Saba, or St Martin. On Barbados, for example, you find the chattel houses – simple huts fashioned out of planks with wide shutters and corrugated roofs built to a basic formula by Bajans living in the country. Short of a caravan, the chattel offers the ultimate in mobility; it is not unusual to see one being moved on the back of a lorry. Yet, common though they may be, no two are ever the same. It is this individuality, expressed in colour or achitectural detail that one finds in the countryside throughout the islands and in the bigger, more permanent buildings in town.

Island estates and their plantation houses are even greater monuments to personal style and expression. The money that was made from the sugar plantations in the days of slavery was often ploughed into the creation of these elegant stone palaces, the grandest

buildings on the island. Many of them are now historic hotels, some of them are in private hands. Often, however, a local society or national trust will organise visits to the oldest and grandest houses on an island and no such opportunity should be missed to catch such an evocative glimpse of the island's past.

Light, colour and beautifully made architectural details all contribute to the appeal of Caribbean buildings

Saba

Saba (pop. 1,000) is one of the strangest, quirkiest islands in the region. Imagine a place where, when you get to the Bottom, you are still 240m above sea level. With its sister St Eustatius and bigger sister St Maarten, Saba is part of the Windward group (Bovenwindse Eilanden) of the Dutch Antilles. It is a member of the Kingdom of the Netherlands, represented at the Antillean parliament in Curaçao.

Nearly every house on the island is whitewashed, with a red roof, red or green shutters and a white picket fence. From the air, it looks like some kind of quaint Legoland, set on 13 sq km of dark green, long-dead volcano rising sharply from the sea.

THE BOTTOM

The Bottom is the capital of the island. In the early days of settlement it was considered safe from attackers, nestling in what was thought to be the bottom of a crater (hence its name). The first settlers used to carry supplies to the village from the harbour, climbing the 500 steps from Ladder Bay, and the adventurous tourist can follow them today. The Bottom is now the home of the island's administrative offices and what few shops there are.

HELL'S GATE

One of the joys of Saba is simply driving round the island. In the 1930s engineers were sent from Holland to investigate the possibility of building a road. Accustomed to the flat expanse of the Netherlands they shook their heads and declared it impossible, much to the chagrin of one Lambertus Hassell, who sent away for lessons in engineering and started building the road by correspondence course. Twenty years later it was finished – a 16km joy-ride of a road, climbing, twisting, falling like the track of a roller coaster. At one point it even splits itself in two to swerve round a tree. Beyond Hell's Gate, in the northeast of the island, there are no less than 20 hairpin bends on the way to the airport. Hassell's skill was great, and no-one has attempted to add more than minor flourishes since.

MOUNT SCENERY

There are several hiking trails, including the Stairwell, a path of 1,064 steps from Windwardside through dense tropical vegetation to the top of Mount Scenery. Here grow giant elephant ears, liannas and ferns, mango and banana trees, wild orchids and heliconias. Some of the vegetation has been labelled to help identification. A short cut for the less ambitious involves taking a taxi to

Red and white are the favourite colours for Saba houses

Rendezvous and joining the path from there.

SABA MARINE PARK

Saba is reputed to have no beaches (although the locals will reluctantly admit to one small, inaccessible strip of sand), so its main attraction for visitors is diving. The Saba Marine Park Foundation, established in 1987, encircles the entire island, and 29 permanent mooring buoys are available for divers' boats. The water is warm, the underwater life is fascinating and visibility is outstanding.
Harbour office, Fort Bay (tel: 463–295).
Open: Monday to Friday, 8am–5pm.

WINDWARDSIDE

The island's second town seems to cling to its hillside, almost 600m above sea level. It is a charming place to explore, with its winding alleys and clusters of classic Saban cottages. The Church of St Paul's Conversion dominates the town with its distinctive red and white steeple.

Saba Museum

This small 150-year-old house has been arranged as it would have been a century ago when it was a sea captain's dwelling. Exhibits include Amerindian axeheads, an old organ and a heavy mahogany four-poster bed with traditional pineapple motifs. Outside there is a bust of Simon Bolivar, who recruited Saban men in 1816 for his fight against Spanish rule in South America.
Open: Monday to Friday, 10am–3pm.
Admission free; donations.

St Eustatius

There was a time when St Eustatius, more commonly called Statia (pop. 1,800), boasted one of the most prosperous ports in the Caribbean. Imagine the combined duty-free business of St Thomas and St Maarten put together, only here the business was conducted in ammunition and arms, tobacco, cotton and slaves. Unfortunately the island's most notable moment of glory also proved to be its downfall: it was the first country anywhere in the world to recognise the newly independent United States of America – and was ultimately sacked by the British navy for the impertinence.

ORANJESTAD

The capital of the island consists of a Lower Town and an Upper Town, separated by a 35m bluff. Lower Town is the site of most of the old ruined warehouses from the days when the island was referred to as the Golden Rock. There are plans to renovate some and convert them into tourist attractions. Upper Town is the site of much long-term archaeological excavation by students from William and Mary's College in America. The main streets of this part of the town are soon to be stripped back to their original paving stones. A guided walk through town starts from the museum.

Once St Eustatius was very rich, now it is poor – hence the billboard encouragement

Fort Oranje

The two areas of Oranjestad are connected by a steep path known as Slave Road or, more colloquially, Cardiac Arrest. This leads to Fort Oranje where the 18th-century Governor de Graff fired his famous salute; in its courtyard there is a plaque marking the event, presented by President Roosevelt in 1939. The fort has been extensively restored, although a recent fire destroyed one of the principal buildings. There are plans here to open an interpretation centre.

Upper Town. Open access.

STATIA'S LITTLE BLUE BEADS

There can be precious few left, but people strolling along the Strand in front of Oranjestad are still finding the little blue beads used in the purchase of slaves. Collect enough for a line from the top of your middle finger to your wrist and you have a *bitel*. Put together four *bitels* to form a *khete*, and you have the 18th-century price of a very young slave.

House and shop in Oranjestad

St Eustatius Museum

A visit to the Simon Doncker House is the essential prelude to a stroll through Oranjestad. This is the headquarters of the Sint Eustatius Historical Foundation and contains an excellent museum of island artefacts. Part of the house is also furnished in the style of the St Eustatius of the 19th century.

12 Van Tonningenweg (tel: 32 2288). Open: Monday to Friday, 9am–5pm; weekends, 9am–noon. Admission charge.

THE QUILL

There are at least a dozen nature trails around Statia, the most rewarding of which leads up the island's outstanding landmark, the Quill, the rim of a dormant volcanic crater nearly 300m across. From Welfare Road it takes about 45 minutes to climb up the often slippery track, and another 30 to slither back down. Inside is a luxuriant rainforest of mahogany, breadfruit and cotton trees, tangled with mosses and ferns. The view from the highest point of the rim, known as Mazinga, is certainly worth the rigours of the climb.

STATIA'S ALLIANCE

On 16 November 1776 the American brig-o-war, the *Andrew Doria,* sailed into the busy harbour firing its 13 guns to indicate America's long-sought independence. Governor Johannes de Graff ordered the 11 guns at Fort Oranje to be fired in reply, and Statia became known as 'America's Childhood Friend'. The event is still celebrated in an annual festival. What is not celebrated is the later attack on the ships and warehouses of the port by the British Admiral Rodney.

St Kitts

The Carib Indians called this island Liamuiga, the Fertile Land, and it is not hard to understand why, at the sight of sweeping fields of sugar cane beneath lush green hills. Christopher Columbus changed its name in 1493 to that of his patron saint, St Christopher (a name British settlers later shortened to St Kitts). It was not until 130 years later that the first British colony was established on what later became known as the 'mother colony' to all the other British possessions in the Caribbean. For a while the village of Half-Way Tree marked the agreed division of the island between Britain and France until the Treaty of Versailles in 1783 handed over full control to Britain. St Kitts and her sister island Nevis became independent in 1983.

BASSETERRE

The capital, Basseterre, owes its name to the years of shared rule with France. It is a typical Caribbean town of gingerbread-trimmed houses built half with stone, half with timber. The magnetic centre of town is the Circus, where traffic circulates round an ornate painted clock tower, the **Berkeley Memorial**, crafted in honour of a former president of the island's legislative council.

Independence Square, built in 1790 and known until 1983 as Pall Mall Square, in the east of the town, was once a busy slave market and site of the island's council meetings. It is surrounded by restored Georgian houses.

Well-preserved, Basseterre is a pleasant and rewarding place to explore

BLOODY POINT

One of the most violent chapters in St Kitts' history unfolded at Bloody Point at the mouth of the Stone Fort River. On learning from a Carib girl that her countrymen were planning an attack on the foreign settlers in 1626, Sir Thomas Warner organised a joint force of British and French soldiers to stamp out the rebellion. It is said that 2,000 Caribs were slaughtered at this place and that the blood flowed for three days afterwards.
Near the village of Challengers, northwest of Basseterre.

BRIMSTONE HILL

Known as the Gibraltar of the West, Brimstone Hill is one of the most important and best-preserved fortresses in the Caribbean. As is often the case here, its history is the story of the struggle between France and Britain. The first cannons were mounted on this site in 1690 by British troops in an effort to capture Fort Charles (now in ruins near the coast) which was held by the French. In January 1782, when it was still only partially completed, French soldiers besieged the fort. Less than 1,000 British soldiers held out for a month before surrendering on 12 February. Eventually Fort Brimstone was returned to Britain under the Treaty of Versailles.

Situated 250m above the Caribbean, the fortress allows visitors a superb view across to the neighbouring islands before a self-guided tour leads them through the restored buildings: the officers' quarters, the ordnance store, the Prince of Wales bastion and the Citadel, where the Fort George Museum is housed.
Approximately 22km northwest of Basseterre on the Main Road. Open: Monday to Saturday, 9.30am–5.30pm, Sunday 9.30am–4pm. Admission charge.

ROMNEY MANOR

A popular stop on most tourist itineraries, Romney Manor is a 17th-century greathouse and plantation set in 2 hectares of tropical gardens. Many people set off on hikes into the rainforest near by. Largely unspoilt, the forest is full of orchids and other flowers, as well as birds of many species. The manor is home to a famous local batik and textile business and most visitors come to shop.
1km west of Road Town on the Main Road northwest of Basseterre (tel: 465 6253). Open: Monday to Saturday, 9am–5pm. Admission charge.

THE SOUTHEAST PENINSULA

Recently opened to traffic, the peninsula which trails like a kite's tail from the island offers good views of the islands to the south. The best beach on the island is here at Friar's Bay.

Nevis

A short 19km, 45-minute ferry ride from St Kitts, Nevis (pop. 9,000) is one of the most relaxed and relaxing islands in the Caribbean. A 93 sq km lush green volcanic cone rising to 900m above the sea, it rather inevitably owes its name to Christopher Columbus; seeing the summit of the mountain covered with clouds and spotting a likeness to the snow-capped mountains of Europe, he was moved to name the island Nuestro Señora de las Nieves, Our Lady of the Snows.

Although the earliest settlers brought tobacco to plant on the island, by the 18th century sugar had become the white gold of the Caribbean, bringing great wealth to the owners of the 86 sugar plantations of Nevis.

CHARLESTOWN

Located on Gallows Bay on the west side of the island, Charlestown is the bustling commercial capital of Nevis. There are some classic examples of colonial Caribbean architecture here, particularly on Main Street and around Walwyn Plaza. Close to the town's pier the Cotton Ginnery is still used to comb cotton every spring.

Alexander Hamilton House Museum

The birthplace of the famous American statesman, the first Secretary of the American Treasury (1755–1804), this house was originally built in 1680 but was later destroyed, probably by an earthquake. It is therefore a more recent Georgian-style building which houses the Hamilton Museum. There are Amerindian artefacts, a display of contemporary photographs of island life and an illustrated history of Hamilton himself.

Low Street. Open: Monday to Friday, 8am–4pm; Saturday, 8am–noon.

BATH HOTEL AND SPRING HOUSE

In its heyday, the Bath Hotel was one of the most fashionable health spas and resorts in the world. Built in 1778, it made use of the nearby sulphur springs to provide medicinal baths which were said to be beneficial for all sorts of ailments. Within 60 years, however, the hotel was closed and the building had fallen into neglect. Today, anyone curious about the restorative properties of the springs can still take a dip in the old bathhouse in the hotel grounds. There are five baths with temperatures varying from 40° to 42°F.

Approximately 800m south of Charlestown. Open: daily, 9am–4pm. Admission charge.

STAMPS

Philatelists are attracted to the range of colourful stamps issued regularly in the Caribbean. They are highly collectable and most islands have a central philatelic bureau which will send first day covers of new stamps abroad on payment of a standing order.

The Nevis Philatelic Bureau, Main Street, Charlestown. Open: Monday and Tuesday, 8am–4.30pm, Wednesday and Friday, 8am–4pm, Thursday 8am–noon.

Quintessential tropical beach: Pinney's

HORATIO NELSON MUSEUM

The Nevis island council has recently built a museum to house its collection of Lord Nelson memorabilia. Nelson, admiral of the British naval fleet based in Antigua and later hero of the Battle of Trafalgar, was first attracted to Nevis by the prospect of fresh water for his ships. Then he met and married Fanny Nisbet, widow of a wealthy plantation owner. The museum has an exhibition entitled 'Nevis in the Time of Nelson'.

Belle Vue (tel: 469 0408). Open: Monday to Friday, 9am–4pm; Saturday, 10am–noon. Admission charge.

PINNEY'S BEACH

This 6km long stretch of white sand, backed by a profusion of multi-angled palm trees, is one of the finest beaches in the Caribbean and epitomises most people's vision of this tropical region. Those keen on watersports are well catered for.

Just north of Charlestown.

ST JOHN'S ANGLICAN CHURCH

Originally built in 1680, the small village church proudly displays the official register of Admiral Nelson's wedding to Fanny Nisbet in 1787. The signature of Britain's Prince William Henry, later King William IV, who gave the bride away, can also be seen in the register. Lift an edge of carpet in the aisle and a row of tombs is revealed.

Fig Tree village, south of Charlestown. Open access.

Antigua and Barbuda

ANTIGUA

For many people Antigua represents everything they could ask of a Caribbean island; sand, sea, sun and shopping. Perhaps the inland scenery can be a little dull and the roads could certainly be improved, but for a few days of rest and relaxation beside the pool, with a chance to learn windsurfing or to go parascending, there is nowhere better.

Antigua is the largest of the Leeward Islands, formed mostly of limestone with the remains of volcanic activity in one small corner only – where one finds the island's lushest vegetation. Elsewhere it has a rather scrubby look which turns dry and brown during long hot spells. Its Carib name was Wadadli, but when Columbus sailed by in 1493 he called it Santa Maria de la Antigua, after the virgin saint of the Cathedral of Seville. Ultimately it was British settlers from St Kitts who established a colony in Old Town and, apart from a brief occupation of the island for a few months by the French in 1666 and having received statehood in 1967, Antigua stayed British until full Independence in 1981.

ST JOHN'S

For the tourist at least, St John's, the capital of Antigua, has been transformed beyond measure over the last few years with the introduction of new port facilities, restaurants, hotels and, particularly, duty-free shops. Meanwhile,

ANTIGUA

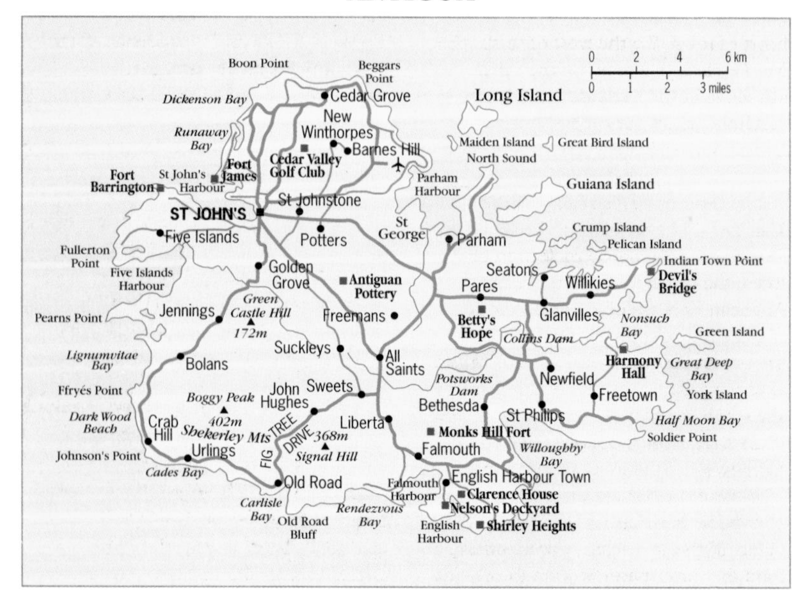

Detail merging into night at St John's Harbour

however, the residents wonder when they are going to see a similar sum spent on their city's infrastructure.

St John's was laid out to a formal design in 1702 and the most interesting areas fall within a six-block grid in the heart of town. To the west of this is the Marketplace, perhaps not the most attractive in the Leeward Islands but certainly one of the liveliest, on a Saturday morning at least.

Cathedral Church of St John the Divine

Dominating the northern section of town, the principal building of the Anglican Diocese of Antigua, and the island's national monument, is a large grey stone building with twin spires and silvery cupolas. The first building on the site was a wooden church built in 1683, while a later stone building started in 1745 was destroyed by an earthquake. The current structure dates back to 1845. The life-size iron figures on the pillars of the south gates, representing St John the Baptist and St John the Divine, are said to have been captured from one of Napoleon's warships. Immediately behind the Cathedral is **Government House**. Originally two separate 17th-century houses, it was bought by Lord Lavington of Carlisle Estate in 1801. Today it is the official residence of the Governor-general of Antigua.
Long Street (tel: 461 0082). Open access.

LORD NELSON

Antigua's most celebrated resident during the time of the battles between the British and the French was Horatio Nelson. In 1784 he took command of the Leeward Island Squadron in which the future British King William IV served as captain of HMS *Pegasus*. The island became the headquarters of the British Royal Navy in the Americas and English Harbour became a strongly fortified haven for British ships. It remains one of the most fascinating and popular historical sites in the Caribbean.

Luxury cruise ship at Redcliffe Quay

Museum of Antigua and Barbuda
St John's first interpretative museum was established by the Historical and Archaeological society of the islands in 1988. It chose, for its home, the Old Court House, the oldest structure still in use on Antigua. Built in 1750, it was the work of an English-born American architect, Peter Harrison, who had helped the governor of Massachusetts to capture Louisburg in 1745. The distinctive white stone of its façade was quarried from an island off Antigua's northeast coast, although it has been repaired and extensively rebuilt over the centuries. It housed the island's parliament until damaged in an earthquake in 1974.

The museum's primary objectives are research and education and many of its displays are of the 'hands on' type designed with children in mind. One of the displays is computer-driven and quizzes visitors on the island's history. But despite its worthy educational aims, the museum's most-prized exhibit is probably still Viv Richards' cricket bat.
Church Street (tel:463 1060). Open: Monday to Thursday, 8.30am–4pm; Friday, 8.30am–3pm; Saturday, 10am–2pm. Admission free.

Redcliffe Quay
A group of former warehouses and other nautical buildings has been carefully restored on the west side of St John's. Although they have been converted into boutiques, restaurants and offices, their original architecture and style have been cleverly preserved. Near by in St Mary's Street, the Central Methodist Church, damaged by an earthquake in 1974, has also been restored to its original condition.

BETTY'S HOPE
Ruined sugar mills are a common sight in Antigua. The remains of two of the most important mills as well as the arches of a boiling house, can still be found at Betty's Hope Plantation. It was established in 1674 by Christopher Codrington, who came to Antigua from Barbados to introduce large-scale sugar production to the island.
Near Pares Village, southeast of St John's.

DEVIL'S BRIDGE
Close to the driest part of the island, Indian Town Point, on the northeast coast, Devil's Bridge is a popular tourist stop. It is a natural limestone arch which has been created over the sea by the pounding of the surf. Many slaves took their own lives here in the 18th century, believing they were cursed by the devil.
1·5km east of Indian Town.

PARHAM HARBOUR
One of the original settlements of the 17th century, Parham Harbour provides a well-protected anchorage for yachts and local fishing boats. The most important building in town is St Peter's Anglican Church, more popularly known just as Parham Church. Built in the 1840s by the architect Thomas Weekes, its octagonal shape makes it particularly interesting.
On the northeast coast of the island. Open access.

SOUTHWEST ANTIGUA
The most scenic area on the island is tucked into its south west corner. Fig Tree Drive, between the village of John Hughes and Old Road, is a fertile, verdant route through tropical vegetation and what is referred to locally as Antigua's rainforest (but which seems to be mainly mango trees and banana groves). The little village of Urlings, northwest of Old Road, clings to the side of Boggy Peak (402m), the highest point on the island, and overlooks Cades Bay. Cades Bay Reef is part of a national park.

The traditional form of haulage on Antigua

THE SOUTHERN HARBOURS

English Harbour

One of the very best natural harbours in the Caribbean, English Harbour was home to the British Admiralty in the West Indies. It was from here that Nelson and Rodney ventured forth to wreak havoc on the French Navy throughout the 18th century.

Their naval base, constructed between 1725 and 1746, occupied the narrow promontory between Falmouth and English Harbour. A series of fortifications was added at the harbour and on the slopes surrounding it, while the western side of the harbour was comprehensively covered by Fort Berkeley whose cannons provided the main defence for Nelson's Dockyard.

All this can be viewed most clearly from the fortifications on Shirley Heights. (See also page 56.)

Falmouth Harbour

The port of Falmouth, in a sheltered bay to the south of the island, was once Antigua's capital and still provides safe anchorage for ships of all kinds. It is surrounded by former sugar plantations, while restored St George's Church stands on the site of a church used by troops in Nelson's day.

Take the main road southeast of St John's.

ANTIGUA'S BEACHES

According to the island's marketing department, Antigua boasts 365 beaches, one for every day of the year. Miraculously, however, it always seems to find another one for leap years. Certainly, there are numerous very good strips of sand.

All the island's beaches are public, but some seem more accessible than others.

Looking down on English Harbour

Dark Wood Beach
The best of the truly public beaches (once spookily known as Dead Sands), this is beside the main road on the southwest coast. There is a beach bar and somewhere to get changed. It can get crowded, particularly on Sundays.

Dickenson Bay
The best-known strip of sand is Dickenson Bay, on the coast road north of St John's. However this is very much a resort beach, with hotels, bars and restaurants along most of its length.

Fort James
The closest beach to the capital. There is parking available, a beach bar and it is popular with locals, but ocean currents can make swimming tricky.

Johnson's Point
Also known as Crab Hill Bay, this is another excellent roadside beach.

BARBUDA

Located 42km north of Antigua, Barbuda is a beachcomber's dream. Apart from miles of soft pink sand, there is little else except turtles, deer, pigs and a small population of just over 1,000 people. Most of the island consists of a near-flat plain rising little more than a few metres above sea-level. The rest, called the Highlands, doubtless by someone with a good sense of humour, rises to all of 40m. Virtually the whole coastline is fringed with coral reefs.

COASTAL WATERS

A large estuary called Codrington Lagoon, along the west coast of the island, is popular with birdwatchers. The island's 170 species include the frigate birds who come in their thousands to breed every autumn. The island's best pink beaches are in the area of Palmetto Point while, off shore, Palaster Reef has been established as a marine reserve.

CODRINGTON

While the Spanish knew of Barbuda's existence in the 16th century, the first attempts to settle the island were made by the British in 1628 and a colony was established where the village of Codrington now stands. This was named after the most powerful family on the island – the Codrington sugar estates were synonymous with the fortunes of the island.

MARTELLO TOWER

There are few historical remains on the island, but a ruined Martello fort and tower can be seen near the village of Dulcina. These served as signal and lookout stations, not just for potential attacks, but also for spotting shipwrecks whose salvage provided additional income.

BARBUDA

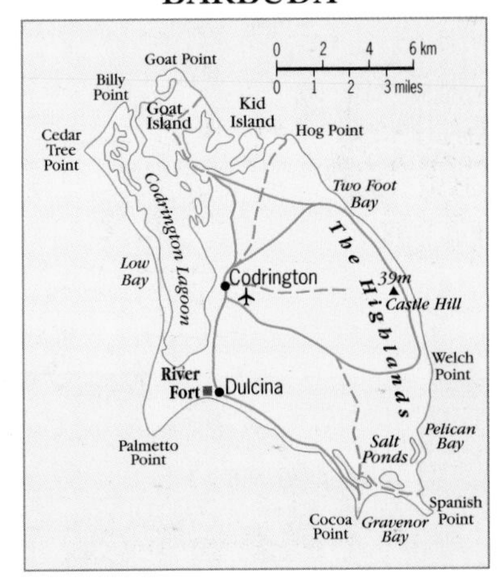

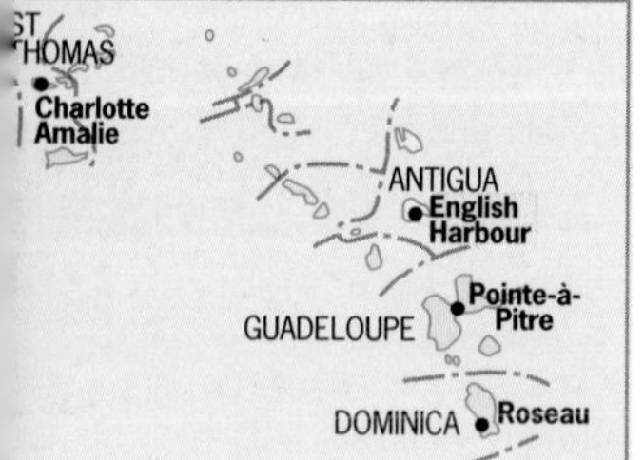

Naval Antigua

Part drive, part walk, this tour starts at Shirley Heights, so if you do not have your own vehicle you will have to hire a taxi from the Dockyard for the short preliminary journey. *Allow two hours.*

1 SHIRLEY HEIGHTS

This vantage point offers a superb view over the historical south of Antigua. Although the name actually belongs to the bluff overlooking the harbour, it is also used for the surrounding ruins of gun emplacements, magazines and military buildings. The construction of the fort, named after General Sir Thomas Shirley, Governor of the Leeward Islands, was begun in 1781 and continued for about 10 years. The first part of the complex to be reached, the Royal Artillery Quarters, contains a small museum with maps and exhibits illustrating the fort's history.

Pause for refreshment at Shirley Heights Lookout then follow the signs to Dow's Hill.

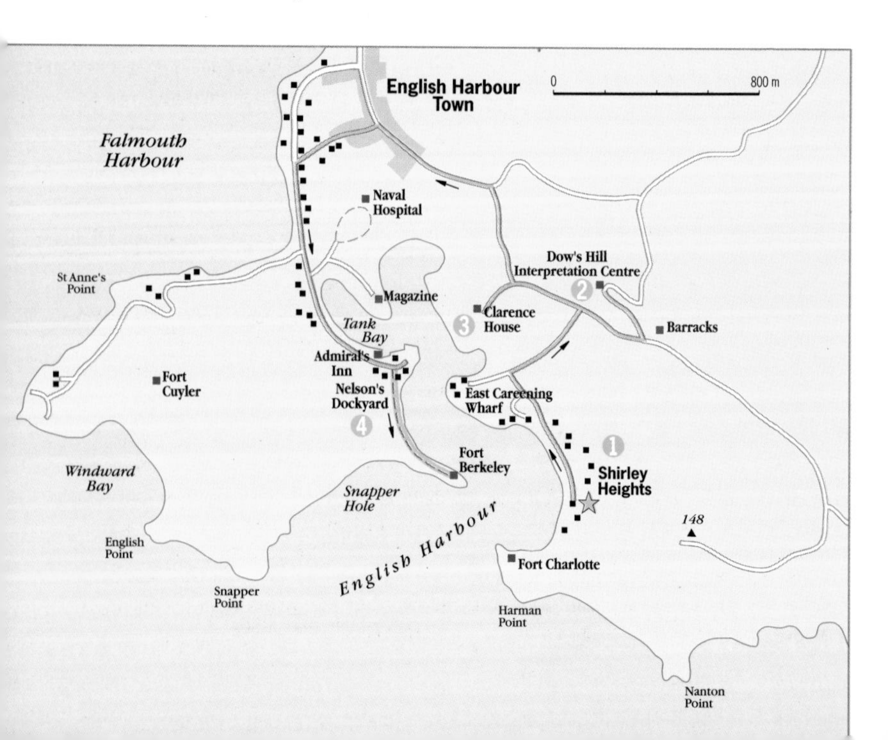

2 DOW'S HILL

Dow's Hill Interpretation Centre is one of Antigua's most recent tourist attractions. A belvedere with interpretative panels guides the viewer round English Harbour, while inside the centre itself there is an auditorium with a multi-media presentation of Antigua's history. There is also a gift shop and a tea room.

Drive down the hill to Clarence House.

3 CLARENCE HOUSE

This is currently the country residence of Antigua's Governor-General, but previously it was home to Prince William Henry, Duke of Clarence, later King William IV of Britain, who was based at English Harbour as commander of HMS *Pegasus* in 1786–7. The Georgian manor, furnished with antiques loaned by the Britain's National Trust, is decorated in period style.

Retrace your steps to the top of the road and turn left for English Harbour Town. From the town follow the signs for Nelson's Dockyard.

4 NELSON'S DOCKYARD

This is a superb example of a Georgian Dockyard and the only one in existence today. It was started in 1743, with construction continuing, off and on, until 1800. Although it carries the name of Britain's most famous admiral, Nelson actually had no part in its development.

From the entrance, walk through the covered area of shops, passing a bank, a post office and various T-shirt sellers. The first building of interest, now known as the Admiral's Inn, used to be the Engineers Office with the pitch and tar store below; the pillars in the dock are all that remain of the old boat house. As you leave and move through the gates into the dock proper what is now a bank on the right used to be the old Guard House and Porter's Lodge. On the left is the Boat House and Joiner's Loft from 1778, where the ships' boats were repaired. The museum and gift shop are housed in the 1855 residence of the naval officer in charge. The Copper and Lumber Store Hotel provided accommodation for seamen whose ships were being careened, while the Officer's Quarters is where they were billeted during the hurricane months. Relax in Limey's and watch the yachts in the harbour or, if you still have energy, take the trail from the dinghy dock to the remains of Fort Berkeley.

Part of so-called Nelson's Dockyard

Shirley Heights Lookout and the Dow's Hill Interpretation Centre are both open daily, 9am–5pm. The opening hours of Clarence House depend on whether or not the Governor-General is in residence. Nelson's Dockyard is open daily, all day. There is an admission charge for all attractions.

Montserrat

*T*he moment the immigration officer stamps a large green shamrock on a visitor's passport it is clear this is somewhere a little bit unusual. It may be just a short 15-minute hop with LIAT from Antigua, but Montserrat looks completely different. There are no white-sand beaches, just black volcanic shores; the dry, flat scrubby land has given way to green volcanic slopes; and the donkey and his rider encountered on the quiet road leading from Montserrat's airport seem light years away from the traffic of St John's.

The Emerald Isle

The reason for the shamrock is that Montserrat, the Emerald Isle, was once colonised by Irish Roman Catholics who were uneasy living on the mainly Protestant island of St Kitts. Montserrat's reputation as a Roman Catholic sanctuary spread and settlers came from as far as Ireland itself to set up their homes. By 1651 there were as many as 1,000 Irish families inhabiting the island. Although it is now a British Crown Colony, the old Irish legacy can still be seen wherever you go; in the names of places and streets (Galways Plantation, Cork Hill, Fogarthy), and people (O'Rourke and O'Reilly), in the shamrock carved above Government House, and in the island's flag itself which may have a Union Jack in one

Memorial-cum-clocktower in Plymouth

corner but also boasts the legendary Erin of Ireland holding a cross and an Irish harp.

PLYMOUTH

The capital of the island is a sleepy sort of place. In the heat of the midday sun the faded paintwork on its old colonial buildings gives it a sort of Wild West look. About a third of the island's 12,500 population live here and this is where the main stores are, although a stroll round the major tourist shops does not take very long.

Fort St George

A good view of the town can be had from St George's Hill. Fort St George was the last fort built on the island, probably around the 1780s. Although there are still several cannons at the summit, most of the battlements are now overgrown.

In addition to its defensive role, the hill was also used to give warning when a hurricane was about to strike the island: two rockets were fired, three cannons were let off and then the church bells of the town would sound a 10-minute alarm.

Reached from Highway 4, to the north of the town.

Government House

Government House is the best-known attraction in Plymouth. It sits in beautifully landscaped gardens, an ornate Victorian mansion looking for all the world like a set for Gilbert and Sullivan's operetta, *The Pirates of Penzance*. The home of the governor of the island, it also contains collections of island artefacts, antique furniture and works of art as well as a superb new wooden floor laid down by a work party from the town's prison.

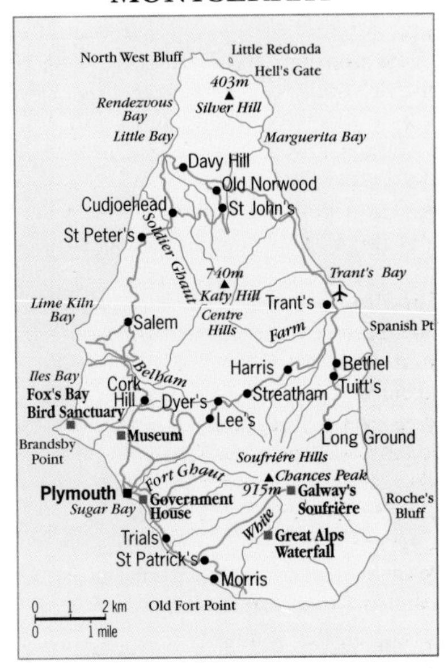

South Plymouth. Free guided tours of the house and gardens take place on Monday, Tuesday, Thursday and Friday, between 10.30am and 12noon.

A tot of bush (spiced) rum, a traditional Caribbean tipple

Antique ordnance at Government House

Montserrat Museum
Housed in the mill of a former sugar plantation, the museum covers Montserrat's history from pre-Columbian times to the present day. There are also displays of the island's natural history and philatelists will appreciate the comprehensive collection of Montserrat's stamps.
Richmond Hill, northeast of Plymouth (tel: 491 5443). Open: Wednesday and Saturday, 2.30pm–5pm, and by special arrangement. Donations.

Plymouth Jail
Like many Caribbean towns, Plymouth keeps its prison in the centre of the town where everybody can see it. It was built in 1664 and is as sturdy as it looks. But do not be surprised to meet a gang of prisoners in the street. They frequently form work parties tidying up the island and working on government projects.

St Anthony's Church
While the Irish celebrated mass in St Patrick's, the English settlers worshipped in St Anthony's Anglican Church, which has a similar history of destruction and resurrection. The stone tablets embedded in its walls provide a fascinating insight into the lives of British families on Montserrat in the 18th and 19th centuries.
Church Street. Open access.

St Patrick's Church
St Patrick's Roman Catholic Church took six years to build and was completed in 1848. It was rebuilt twice however, after hurricanes, but is still one of the most imposing structures in the town and contains interesting pieces of religious art.
George Street. Open access.

FOX'S BAY
Fox's Bay Bird Sanctuary is a 6-hectare wildlife park of mangroves and nesting

areas for gallinules, coots, herons and other waterfowl. There are marked nature trails leading round the sanctuary to the beach and into the interior.
5km northwest of Plymouth. Admission free.

GALWAY'S ESTATE

These are the much-visited remains of a large 520 hectare sugar plantation developed in the 1660s and owned by the Galway family of County Cork, a sugar dynasty which owned estates on several islands. The buildings, now in ruins, are reckoned to date from the mid-1700s and consist of a Georgian-style greathouse, the boiling house, a windmill, a cattle mill, a rum still and two reservoirs, water diversion tunnels and the slave village.

A study of the plantation began in 1981 under the aegis of the Montserrat National Trust, and then in 1990 it was selected by the Smithsonian Institute in the US as a preservation project for the Columbus Quincentennial. The aim of the ongoing work is to develop the site as an historic and cultural centre reflecting plantation life on Montserrat in the 18th century.
5km south of Plymouth. Admission free.

GALWAY'S SOUFRIERE

Rising some 500m above sea level, Galway's Soufrière is the most accessible of several volcanic craters in the mountainous south of the island. The climb to its fuming sulphur vents takes about 20 minutes from the road, but it is worth it for an awesome view of boiling mud, hissing steam and spouting rocks. Although this is a regular stopping point on island tours, it is essential to keep to the well-worn trails, to wear strong shoes, proper clothes and to place feet carefully.
Turn inland on the southern Old Fort Road, just before St Patrick's.

THE CHANCES POND MERMAID

Climb Chances Peak, at 914m the highest point in the island and you may see the legendary mermaid. If she is combing her hair, steal the comb, run down the mountain before her pet snake catches you and her treasure is yours.

GREAT ALPS WATERFALL

A trek for the adventurous is to the Great Alps Waterfall, south of Soufrière, a 20m cascade of the White River through dark green vegetation into a shallow rocky pool. The 45-minute hike leads through a tropical rainforest of trees and ferns garlanded with yellow heliconia (*Heliconia Caribaea)*, Montserrat's national flower, whose odd-looking flowers lead it to be known as lobster claw.
Close to Galway's Soufrière in the south of the island.

Guadeloupe

Touring Guadeloupe, the visitor soon sees that it is in fact two completely different islands joined together by a bridge. Grande-Terre, to the east, is a flat, dry limestone land, quite densely populated, with considerable tourist development along its white-sand beaches. Basse-Terre on the other hand is a jagged volcanic island with a spine of steep, forested mountains rising to 1,500m. The rainfall is great and spectacular waterfalls cascade through rocky canyons down to its volcanic shores.

The Arawak Indians had named it Karukera, the Land of Beautiful Waters, but when Columbus arrived in 1493 he claimed the island for Spain and named it after the monks of the monastery of Santa Maréa de Guadalupe de Extremadura.

Improvised vegetable stalls at Pointe-à-Pitre

There was no permanent settlement until, under the patronage of Cardinal Richelieu in the 1630s, French businessmen formed La Compagnie des Îles d'Amerique to develop Guadeloupe; but, as a French possession in the Caribbean, it inevitably attracted British interest and was occupied twice, until finally reconquered in 1794. In 1946, Guadeloupe was officially designated a French *département*, becoming a fully fledged region with her satellite islands Marie Galante and Les Saintes, and with the responsibility for St Barthélemy and the French half of St Martin added in 1974.

SLAVERY

Early Europeans found the climate in the Caribbean islands ideal for growing sugar cane. As the industry developed there was considerable demand for labour to work the fields. Slaves were imported from Africa, and a triangular trade route grew up between Europe, West Africa and the West Indies, with slaves being exchanged for goods and ultimately sold for cash. It was an arduous journey and many slaves perished. Those who survived would be fattened up in the last few days before reaching port and auctioned off at the various island markets.

GRANDE-TERRE

POINTE-À-PITRE

Although the town of Basse-Terre in the south is actually the administrative centre of the island, Pointe-à-Pitre is the commercial capital and, with 26,000 inhabitants, the largest city on the island. The narrow streets are busy with shoppers, and cars circulate slowly and endlessly in search of a parking space. Nevertheless, it is worth taking time to look around at the city's colonial architecture.

At the broad **Place de la Victoire** in the centre of town Victor Hugues celebrated his success over the British forces by planting rows of royal palms and sandbox trees, and this is one of the most peaceful parts of Pointe-à-Pitre. While an unseemly sprawl of T-shirt sellers usually occupies the area immediately between the port and the square, the city's **Central Market** near by is a fine, high roofed colonial-style public plaza, where local women sell fruit, vegetables, spices and craftwork.

Close by, the **Musée Schoelcher**, an ornate pink building, is dedicated to the memory of the man who led the successful fight against slavery after Napoleon had reintroduced it in 1802.

Central Market, corner of Peynier and Rue Frebault. Open: Monday to Saturday, 7am–5pm. Musée Schoelcher, 24 Rue Peynier (tel: 82.08.04). Open: Monday to Friday, 9am–noon and 2.30pm–5.30pm. Admission charge.

GUADELOUPE

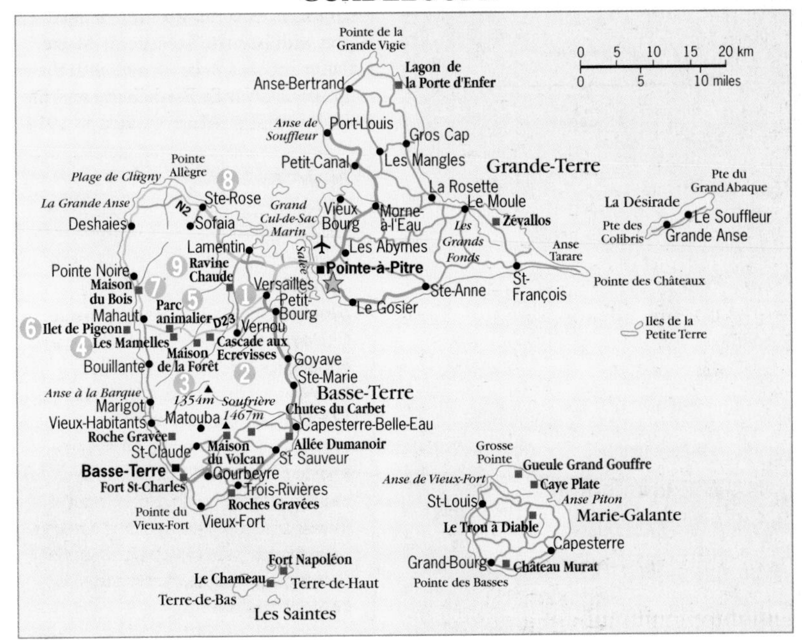

LE MOULE

Grande-Terre, the eastern half of Guadeloupe, is sugar cane country. To appreciate this take any one of the web of minor roads over the little hills and valleys, Les Montagnes Russes, across the island between Les Abymes and Le Moule. A low-rise town spread over a large area of coast, Le Moule used to be the capital of the island and was the site of fierce battles between the Caribs and the early French settlers. Today it is the main town on the rough Atlantic coast.

MUSEE D'ARCHEOLOGIE PRECOLOMBIENNE

The neighbouring village of La Rosette has a collection of Amerindian artefacts gathered from throughout the region.
La Rosette (tel: 235743). Open: Monday, Wednesday to Friday and Sunday, 9.30am–12.30pm and 2.30pm–5.30pm; Tuesday, 10.30am–6.30pm; Saturday, 9.30am–5.30pm. Admission charge.

Plage de la Grand Anse, in the northwest

PETIT-CANAL

At Petit-Canal, the Monument to Liberty stands at the top of 53 steps. Each step represents a sugar plantation which once flourished on Guadeloupe.
On the west coast of Grande-Terre.

POINTE DES CHATEAUX

This is as far as one can go to the east on Grande-Terre and is marked by a large white cross above the rocks. It is a good place to watch the surf rolling in from the Atlantic, crashing against the little offshore islands, Les Iles de la Petite Terre. Immediately before the point a rough track crosses to Tarare Beach, one of the most secluded on the island and popular with naturists.

BASSE-TERRE

BASSE-TERRE

Guadeloupe's administrative capital, the

BEACHES

Grande-Terre has enough beaches for everyone (although those in the area of Le Gosier and Sainte-François tend to become crowded). Try instead the hidden beach at Morne à L'Eau, the sheltered cove at La Porte d'Enfer, or Anse de Souffleur near Port-Louis. Basse-Terre is less well known for its beaches, but try Plage de la Grande Anse near Deshaies or those by Trois-Rivières.

The mayor's residence, Caber Street, Basse-Terre

town of Basse-Terre is a much more relaxed place than Pointe-à-Pitre in the north. Until the early 16th century it was two separate communities divided by the Rivière aux Herbes: the Carmel Quarter, to the south of the river, was the military section surrounding Fort St-Charles, while Saint-François to the north was the more ordered commercial district.

Fort St-Charles

The ramparts of Fort St-Charles occupied a good position at the south end of Basse-Terre. The fort, built in 1650, was enlarged over two centuries. There is a small museum .

At the southern edge of the town. Open: daily, 9am–5pm. Admission free.

CHUTES DU CARBET (CARBET FALLS)

The road which thrusts inland from the village of Saint-Sauveur on the southeastern edge of the island climbs sharply to the impressive, and popular, Carbet Falls. Here the water cascading down the eastern slopes of the volcano is channelled into a series of three waterfalls. The first tumbles 125m down a steep defile, the second drops 110m down a wider gorge, the third falls 20m in a torrent of spray. There are hikes to all three falls, but the second drop is the most dramatic.

Habituée Road, near St-Sauveur.

LA MAISON DU VOLCAN

Up a steep and narrow road 6·5km inland from Basse-Terre, Saint-Claude is a wealthy suburb of old planters' houses in a lush setting of trees and tropical gardens. A visitor centre within the village, La Maison du Volcan, has an exhibition relating to La Soufrière (and particularly its eruption in 1976) and other volcanic regions of the Caribbean.

St-Claude. Open: daily, 10am–6pm. Admission free.

A total of three dramatic falls makes up the waterfall at Carbet

MATOUBA

The village of Matouba was originally settled by indentured workers brought from India in the mid-19th century. It is said that ancient rites, including animal sacrifices, are still practised here.

The hot springs near by are famous throughout the Caribbean for their therapeutic properties.

Matouba is located 3km northwest of St-Claude.

NATIONAL PARK OF GUADELOUPE

Most of Basse-Terre, some 30,000 hectares, is covered and protected by Guadeloupe's national park service. Here there are wild, untouched places and a 400km system of serviced tracks, known as *traces*, which allow the visitor to get close to nature. Facilities for the public are good, with rest and picnic areas and interpretation centres in the most popular areas. The park plays an important educational role as well as spear-heading the conservation efforts in the area. The Grand Cul-de-Sac Marin, for example, is an area of 3,700 hectares which has been set aside to protect the flora and wildlife of the island's coastal swamps.

For more detailed information on the national park and its plant-life, contact the Office National des forêts, Jardin Botanique, Basse-Terre (tel: 81 17 20). *(See also page 68.)*

SOUFRIERE

At 1,467m, Soufrière reaches the highest point among the dark green, deeply creviced mountains which dominate southern Guadeloupe. Nicknamed the Mount St Helen of the Caribbean after its last eruption in 1976, it continues to bubble and burp. Nevertheless it is usually quiet enough to be climbed. Drive as far as La Savane à Mulets, where there are four well-marked colour-coded trails which lead to the summit and its strange and eerie landscape of boiling mud, weird volcanic rocks and steaming pits. It takes approximately two hours to climb this route.

LES SAINTES

A short ferry ride from Trois-Rivières, Les Iles des Saintes should be on every visitor's itinerary – an immensely attractive archipelago of eight little volcanic islands, where passengers arriving from the mainland are traditionally met by local children carrying trays of *tourments d'amour*, coconut tarts. It is certainly hard to imagine this as the setting for one of the fiercest naval battles in the history of the Caribbean: on 12 April 1782 Admiral Rodney and his British forces decisively defeated the French navy at the Battle of Les Saintes. The French, under Commander de Grasse, were sailing to join the Spanish navy at Santo Domingo for an attack on Jamaica, the wealthiest British colony in the Caribbean.

BOURG DES SAINTES

The majority of Les Saintes' population of 3,260 live in the village of Bourg des Saintes, on the island of Terre-de-Haut, a sleepy place of flower-bordered lanes disturbed only by the occasional whine of motor scooters (the island's main form of transportation).

Apart from the opportunity to sit and watch the fishermen racing their famous *santois* fishing boats, the main tourist attractions here are several very good restaurants, shops and craft galleries.

FORT NAPOLEON

It is quite a long hike on a hot day to Fort Napoléon on its hill overlooking Bourg. Built by the French between 1845 and 1867, it was restored in 1975 and a guided tour can be taken round the barracks and the prisoners' cells. There is also a small museum and a little botanical garden.

Open: daily, 8am–noon. Admission charge.

FRENCH INHERITANCE

Most of the people who live on the Saintes are descended from the first sea-faring Norman and Breton settlers. They tend to have fair freckled skin, blue eyes; some have red hair. Many are fishermen who still wear the *salako*, a wide, broad-brimmed straw hat which their ancestors introduced from France.

Spectacular plants are commonplace on Guadeloupe. This is the flower of a ginger plant

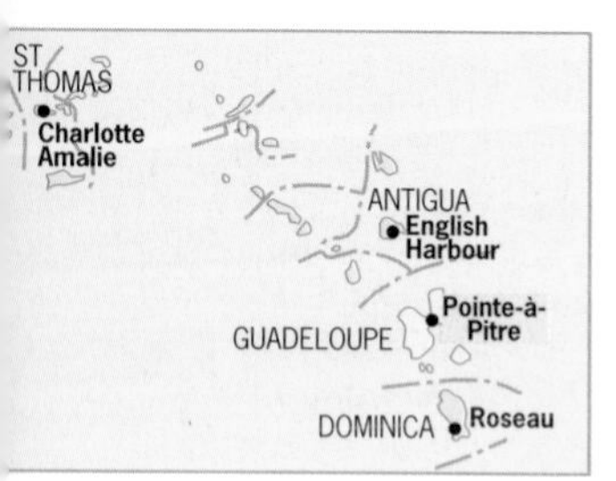

Guadeloupe Drive

A drive which takes in some of the attractions of the national park, including the beautiful Route de la Traversée across the north of Basse-Terre. For the drive route see the main Guadeloupe map on page 63. *Day trip.*

Leave Pointe-à-Pitre by the road south across the bridge to Basse-Terre. At Versailles, take the right-hand slip road on to the D23.

1 LA ROUTE DE LA TRAVERSEE

This is the only road crossing Basse-Terre. It starts among banana and sugar cane fields and climbs to 180m at Vernou, a stylish little residential district of villas overlooking the Lezarde River Valley.

At a steep dip in the road 1km or so after you enter the national park stop at the sign 'Cascade aux Ecrevisses'.

2 CASCADE AUX ECREVISSES

A short 10-minute walk along the banks of the Corossol river, the Cascade aux Ecrevisses is a popular place for a swim or a picnic.

Continue west along the main road and turn in at the sign to Maison de la Forêt.

3 MAISON DE LA FORET

At the side of the road in the Bras David Tropical Park, this information centre is the starting point for a series of colour-coded trails into the rainforest and across the Bras David River.

Staying on the main road, you soon see Les Mamelles.

4 LES MAMELLES

Twin volcanic peaks, these are the most recognisable landmarks in the north of

In the national park

Basse-Terre. This area is renowned for hiking and there is a path to the top of the taller of the two, Mamelle de Pigeon. It is a shorter 30-minute hike to the panoramic viewpoint at 600m.
As the road descends towards the coast you will see a sign on the right-hand side to the botanical park.

5 PARC ANIMALIER

Thanks to the humid climate at this altitude, the Zoological and Botanical Park offers the visitor a chance to stroll through lush tropical vegetation, perhaps seeing racoons, agoutis, iguanas and land turtles.
Follow the road to the coast. There is an optional detour now south to Pigeon Island. Ferries leave for the island from near the road.

6 ILET DE PIGEON

The waters around Pigeon Island make up a protected underwater reserve established by the French diver Jacques Cousteau. Glass-bottom boats leave the dock regularly for the five-minute trip to the island to view the sealife and the reef; snorkellers can hire boats by the hour near by.
Head north towards Pointe Noire.

7 MAISON DU BOIS (HOUSE OF WOOD)

Pointe Noire is the capital of traditional cabinet-making on the island and the House of Wood introduces the visitor to the different kinds of trees and their uses.
Continue along the main road around the northern tip of Basse-Terre.

8 LA MUSEE DU RHUM

Not surprisingly, this museum at the village of Sainte-Rose is a popular tourist destination in the north of Basse-Terre.

Infant bananas

An exhibition, labelled in both French and English, guides you through the history of rum production on the island and the methods of distillation, and ends with a chance to taste the real thing.
Drive carefully towards Lamentin.

9 RAVINE CHAUDE

At the Ravine Chaude in Lamentin natural hot springs have been turned into outdoor swimming pools. The sulphurous waters are reputed to have therapeutic properties. True or not, this is a good place to relax before driving back along the N2 to Pointe-à-Pitre.

Maison de la Forêt, the Zoological and Botanical Gardens, Maison du Bois, la Musée du Rhum and the hot springs are all open daily, 9am–5pm. Admission charge at all, except Maison de la Forêt.

WILDLIFE

While the Caribbean is renowned for its natural beauty, the richness of its wildlife is seldom acknowledged. In the past, this has put several species endemic to the islands at risk by deforestation inland and development of resorts along the coast.

Now, however, conservationists are fighting back; increasing awareness, among both locals and tourists, of the value of each island's natural history has resulted in the establishment of both marine reserves and land-based conservation areas.

No one in Dominica these days can doubt the value of the island's two rare parrots, the Sisserou and the Jaco, or red-necked, parrot; Grenada protects its prized dove by government ordinance; in St Vincent colourful road signs remind people of the penalties for harming the rare St Vincent parrot; and St Lucia's visitors have been intrigued by a bus called the Jacquot Express which, decorated with forest motifs and squawking loudly as it drives through the villages, spreads the message of the importance of the island's birdlife.

'Ecotourists' now also play their part. The cost of visiting or staying in nature centres and retreats throughout the region usually includes a contribution towards conservation work, and visitors often take an active role in monitoring the welfare of species. They may, for example, participate in a bird count in Trinidad, help guard the sea turtles as they come ashore during the nesting season on Antigua, Trinidad or Tobago, or they may even, on behalf of the Department of Conservation in

Left: scarlet ibis
Below left: St Lucia parrot
Above: green turtle arriving to lay eggs
Right: humpback whale
Below: pelican

the British Virgin Islands, photograph and count the humpback whales which travel along Tortola's north shore every spring. Conservationists are pointing to these projects as proof that the development of tourism on the islands and the work to preserve the Caribbean's wildlife need not be mutually exclusive.

Dominica

When the King of Spain asked Christopher Columbus about his newly discovered island of Dominica, the great man is said to have been stumped for words to describe its magnificent mountainous scenery, its rivers and valleys. Apparently he just scrunched up his dinner napkin, dropped it on the table and said 'It looks like this, Your Majesty' – which might not have won any prizes for creativity, but certainly summed up the general shape of this 1,126 sq km island.

The Carib Indians who lived on the island before Columbus were slightly more descriptive than the great explorer. They called the island Wai'tukubuli, meaning 'tall is her body'. Remarkably, the island is still home to about 3,000 of their descendants, who live in a protected area of about 1,500 hectares in the northeast. Here they work the land and continue to practice their traditional skills of canoe building and basket work.

Grandmother, mother and daughter – three generations of Carib Indians

Dominica has managed to avoid the excesses of modern Caribbean tourism simply because it has so few beaches. For many years it also had few hotels and very bad roads. Now, the country's infrastructure has improved and recently tourists have started to come to the island for its fascinating natural history and its wildlife.

ROSEAU

Situated on a flat river delta at the mouth of the Roseau River, the town of Roseau was second choice as the island's capital until Portsmouth, further to the north, was found to be mosquito-ridden and infested with malaria. Not one of the prettiest towns in the Caribbean, Roseau nevertheless has some fine examples of old colonial architecture.

Botanical Gardens

Set on the lower slopes of Morne Bruce, on the outskirts of Roseau, the 16 hectare Botanical Gardens will help nature lovers identify some of the trees and plants they are likely to see around the island. Perhaps the most interesting of the 150 or so species of trees here is the aptly named No-Name tree – scientists have been unable to identify it to date.

East of Roseau (tel: 4482401). Open: daily, 6am–dusk. Admission free.

Roseau Cathedral
The Roman Catholic Cathedral of Our Lady of Fair Haven was built in 1845 and has, incorporated into its sidewalls, a series of old stained-glass windows, one of them depicting Columbus' journeys to the Americas. These contrast with the more modern windows behind the altar.
Virgin Lane. Open access.

Roseau Market
For many people the highpoint of a morning in Roseau is a visit to the market, particularly early on a Friday or Saturday when there is ample proof of the island's natural abundance. This is a comparatively new structure; the original market, where slaves were auctioned off and executions carried out, stood on the square beside the waterfront, now called Dawbiney Market Plaza.
Bay Street. Open: Monday to Saturday, 6am–5pm.

Waterside hotel near Roseau

Last of the sun on Dominica

CABRITS NATIONAL PARK

The forested peninsula of the Cabrits National Park at the northwestern tip of the island, close to Portsmouth, is an important area. Its extensive fortifications are of historical significance and interest, and it also comprises a 320 hectare marine reserve of great natural beauty. An underwater trail, marked with white buoys in the centre of the bay, provides excellent snorkelling, while the coral and rock formations under the steep cliffs on the north side are of interest to divers. The peninsula's southern edge is dominated by Fort Shirley, built by the British between 1770 and 1815 and in its time one of the most impressive military installations in the region. It now serves as an interpretative centre for the whole of the national park.

3·2km north of Portsmouth. Open access to park. Open: daily, 9am–5pm. Admission free.

INDIAN RIVER

One of the most popular tourist distractions on Dominica is a boat trip along the Indian river from Portsmouth, tracing the route the Caribs used, through the mangrove swamps, from the sea to their settlements. The luxuriant vegetation hugs the banks and hangs low overhead, forming a dark green tunnel; Herons fly up from their roosts, crabs scuttle for cover, fish slap back into the water.

Local guides, and their boats, can be found in Portsmouth.

MORNE TROIS PITONS PARK

This 6,800 hectare national park covers

much of the south central portion of the island. Here you find primordial rainforest, **Boeri Lake** and **Freshwater Lake**, **Trafalgar Falls** and **Middleham Waterfall**, the **Boiling Lake** and a hiking trail to the summit of the highest of the Trois Pitons (1,424m).

Laudat is the departure point for many of these attractions. It is from near here, for example, that the **Titou Gorge** leads to the **Valley of Desolation**, an active fumarole area. (Fumaroles are cracks through which gases escape from the molten lava below.) This is also the source of the Boiling Lake, the second largest solfatar lake in the world and a trip not to be undertaken lightly. An easier outing is to the **Emerald Pool**, a clear clean grotto filled by a waterfall and surrounded by tropical plants. A walk down to the Emerald Pool is a popular Sunday afternoon excursion for islanders.

The village of Laudat is 11km east of Roseau. The Emerald Pool is reached from the Castle Bruce road, 5·5km northeast of Pont Cassé. *(See also page 76.)*

NORTHERN FOREST RESERVE

Dominica's highest mountain, the 1,420m Morne Diablotin, is protected within this 8,800 hectare reserve together with the natural habitat of the indigenous and endangered Sisserou and Jaco parrots. It has been proposed to convert the park and another area near by into a national park known as the Morne Diablotin National Park.

PORTSMOUTH

The second town of Dominica, Portsmouth, overlooks Prince Rupert Bay, the best natural harbour on the island. It is a quiet place of just 2,000 inhabitants but was once the scene of one of the most decisive naval battles of the colonial wars, when the British Navy defeated the French in 1782.

LA VIE DOMNIK MUSEUM

Situated in the Old Mill Cultural Centre, this is the island's principal museum. An attractive display describes the island's geographical origins together with its history and the development of the culture of its people.

Near Canefield Airport, north of Roseau.
Open: Monday to Friday, 9am–5pm.

A one-time sugar plantation is the setting for La Vie Domnik Museum

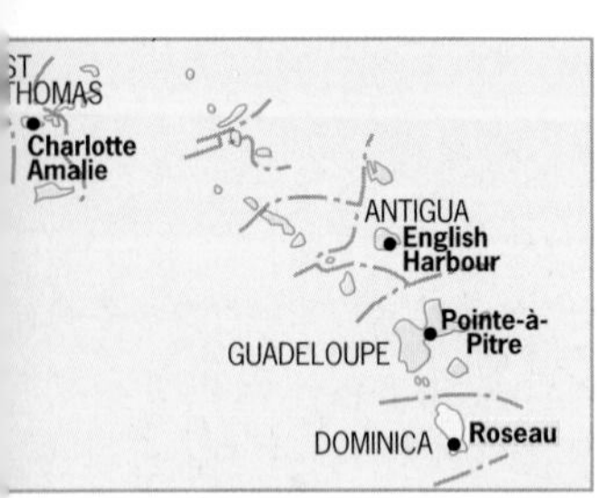

Dominica Drive

This tour takes you through Roseau and into the Morne Trois Pitons National Park. Most of it is by car but, depending on the options taken, there may also be some energetic footwork involved. Take your swimming costume. *Allow 2 hours. Begin from the Old Market Square in Roseau.*

There is an optional stop at the island's Botanical Gardens to see the rare Sisserou and Jaco parrots in their newly built aviaries.

Leave Roseau along King George V Street, cross the Roseau River Bridge up towards the Valley area, and continue to the village of Laudat and Papillote Wildlife Retreat..

1 PAPILLOTE WILDLIFE RETREAT

Papillote Wildlife Retreat was begun beneath Morne Macaque in 1969 by a former New Yorker, Anne Baptiste, as a series of mini-environments designed to meet the needs of assorted indigenous plant groups. The result is a riot of orchids, ferns, aroids and bromeliads. The garden follows the contour of the

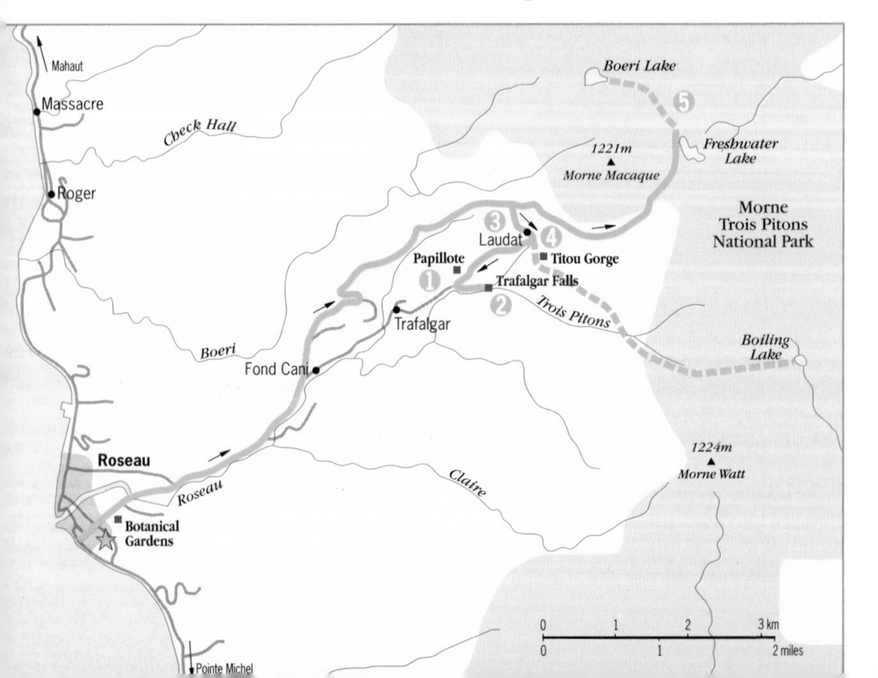

mountainside and is intended as both a wilderness retreat and a nature sanctuary (tel: 44 82287; open access during daylight hours). The 150 or so species of bird which can be seen from Papillote's terraces include Antillean crested hummingbirds, bananaquits, little blue herons, yellow warblers and scaly-breasted thrashers.

Follow the trail to Trafalgar Falls. You may well be asked if you would like a guide to the Falls – most people manage without.

2 TRAFALGAR FALLS

This is one of the most beautiful and accessible sites in the national park. There are actually three separate cascades: a 20-minute hike brings you to the base of Papa Falls, the smaller Mama Falls are to the right and the Baby, the smallest, are on the left. This is where you can put on your swimming costume and enjoy a natural jacuzzi. Slip into the pool and work your way to the left. Here you will see the orange-coloured rocks where the hot springs join the stream. Immerse yourself here – the higher you go, the hotter the water.

Return to Papillote for a well-earned rum punch.

3 LAUDAT

There are several options when you return to Laudat. If you are there bright and early and feel very fit, you could hike the three or four hours to the Boiling Lake. It is spectacular and one of the strangest sights in the Caribbean, but it is also very hard work and you should take a guide.

4 TITOU GORGE

Alternatively, 15 minutes further inland, there is the chance of another refreshing swim at the Titou Gorge. The gorge is

A vista of greenest greens in Morne Trois Pitons National Park

the result of a hydroelectric project based at Trafalgar; there is a smooth water-filled cavern here with a roaring waterfall at its edge.

A rough track leads on to the Freshwater Lake and Boeri Lake.

5 LAKES

The Freshwater Lake at 847m and Boeri Lake at 853m were a single body of water in the crater of an ancient volcano until Morne Macaque formed itself in the crater and separated them. There is a viewpoint beside the Freshwater Lake where you can look down on the east coast of Dominica. If you still have the energy, another hour's hiking takes you up to Boeri Lake.

Otherwise return to Roseau.

Martinique

*T*he Caribs called it Madinina, the Island of Flowers, and they would find little reason to change their minds today. For there is hardly a time of the year when flowers do not grace this island – hibiscus, alamanda, arthuriums, croton, frangipani, poinsettia. Add the thousands of fruit-bearing trees to the picture and at times it seems like another Garden of Eden (but with French drivers).

There are three distinct geographical regions within the island. To the north, steep volcanic mountains are linked by hills called mornes - Pelée in the northeast, the Pitons du Carbet in the centre and Montagne du Vauclin in the south. In the middle of the island the Lamentin Plain, where the island's airport is sited, is the flattest area of land. The southern region features a gentle, hilly landscape and white-sand beaches.

The first French settlers arrived at the mouth of the Roxelane River in about 1630. While the inevitable wrangling over the island between France and Britain continued over the next 150 years, it grew rich on its sugar plantations. Finally restored to France once and for all in 1815, Martinique became an overseas *département* of France in 1946 and achieved regional status in 1974.

Fruit trees on the lower slopes of the cone of Mount Pelée

FORT-DE-FRANCE

There are times, when the sun is setting, the shops are pulling down their shutters, the sea in the bay is turning mauve and flying fish are jumping like sparks from a flint, when the capital of Martinique seems just about the most relaxing place in the Caribbean. There are other times, when you are desperately trying to find a parking space in the middle of the day, when it seems quite the opposite.

Fort-de-France is one of the biggest cities in the region; almost half of the island's population of 360,000 live here. Stretching from the bay of the same name to the foothills of the Pitons du Carbet, it is beautifully positioned. Yet, although the bay is a natural harbour and commercial centre, Fort-de-France did not become the capital until St-Pierre in the north was buried by the eruption of Mount Pelée in 1902.

MARTINIQUE

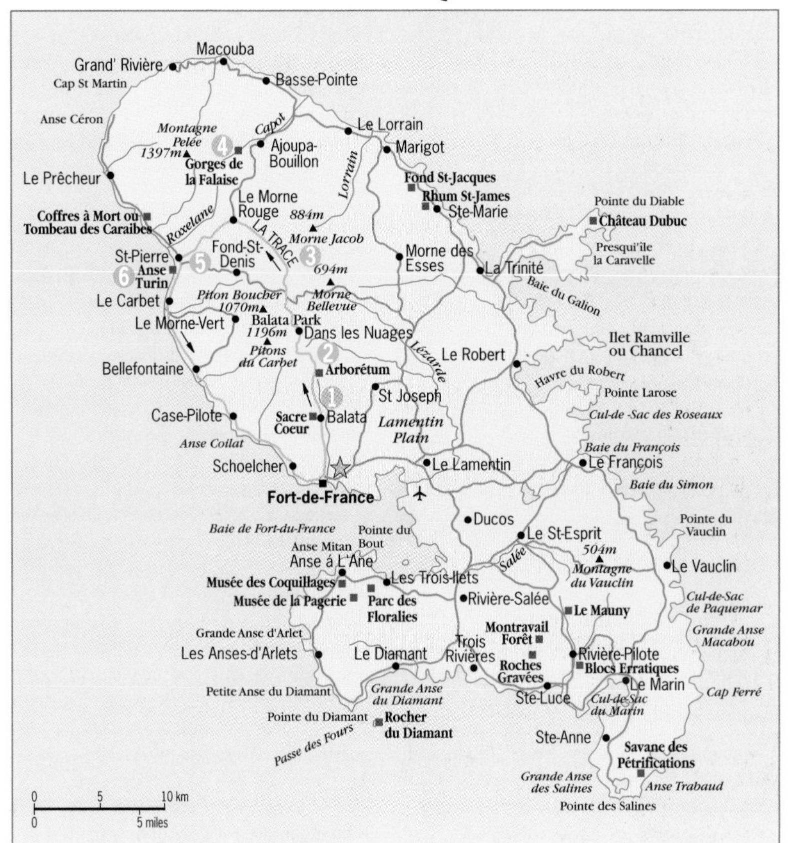

If the heart of the city is **La Savane**, a large grassy public park shaded by flamboyant trees and royal palms, then its soul is probably to be discovered sitting with a *café au lait* outside one of the cafés on its perimeter. La Savane's biggest photo-opportunity, at the northwest corner, is the statue of Marie Josephe Rose Tascher de la Pagerie, better known as Napoleon's **Empress Josephine**, who was born in Les Trois-Ilets across the bay. The white Carrara marble statue by Vital Dubray depicts her in the flowing high-waisted dress of the First Empire (sadly the empress lost her head in suspicious circumstances in 1992 – the city fathers have promised that a new one will be forthcoming in the not-too-distant future). In the meantime, visitors are left to admire her dress and the story of her coronation as depicted in relief around the base.

Earthquake proof? St-Louis Cathedral

Museum of Martinique
Situated on the west side of La Savane, in a beautifully restored colonial house between Fort Saint Louis and the Schoelcher Library, the island's main archaeological museum boasts more than 2,000 artefacts that trace the progressive settlement of the island by the Arawak and Carib peoples. Exhibits include many rare engraved and painted pieces, traditional *ouicou* vases and, notably, a considerable collection of *adornos*. There are also more recent representations of island life, culture, artwork, literature, music, clothing and crafts.
Rue de la Liberté (tel: 71.57.05). Open: Monday to Saturday, 9am–1pm and 2pm–5pm. Admission free.

St-Louis Cathedral
After several other important churches on the site had fallen to natural disasters, the islanders made sure their latest cathedral was earthquake-proof. It was designed in a Romanesque-Byzantine style and finished in 1978, and with its strange metallic spire it resembles a 19th-century church. The stained-glass windows came from the earlier church.
Rue Victor Schoelcher. Open access.

Schoelcher Library
The city's most flamboyant architectural show-piece is to be found at the northwest corner of La Savane. Constructed in Paris in Romanesque-Byzantine style for the Exposition of 1889, the building was then dismantled and shipped, piece by piece, to Martinique where it was rebuilt on a site where the Empress Josephine once lived. It was named after Victor Schoelcher, in recognition of his work as an author and book collector; in 1883, convinced of the need to educate the black population, he donated his entire library of 10,000 books to the country.
Rue de la Liberté. Open: Monday, Tuesday, Thursday 8.30am–12.30 pm and 2pm–6pm; Wednesday and Friday, 8am–1pm; Saturday, 8.30 am–noon. Admission free.

MUSEE DE LA PAGERIE
A small stone building constructed in what was the kitchen of her family estate celebrates the life of the Empress Josephine. Outside, are the ruins of her house, a sugar mill and refinery. Inside, there are artefacts such as her crib, family portraits, personal papers, even a love letter from the Emperor Napoleon. There is a small botanical garden near by called the Parc des Floralies.
Les Trois-Ilets (tel: 68.34.55). Open: Tuesday to Sunday, 9am–5pm. Admission charge.

MARTINIQUE AQUARIUM

With an area of 1,400 sq m and displaying more than 2,000 fish, the Aquarium of Martinique is an impressive sight. The collection, which is particularly devoted to Caribbean marine species, demonstrates the wide range of fauna and flora beneath the sea. A tankful of sharks, however, seems to be the most popular attraction. The Aquaterrarium, within the complex, also displays a cross-section of tropical river life.

Boulevard de la Marne, near Fort-de-France (tel: 73.02.29). Open: daily 9am–7pm. Admission charge.

PLANTATION LEYRITZ

The grounds of the restored plantation house (now a hotel) are open to anyone and a small museum houses dolls made entirely out of vegetables and local plants. Each figurine represents a famous woman of French history (though occasionally it takes a bit of imagination to work out who's who). There is also a sugar factory to visit in the grounds.

Plantation Leyritz in the northeastern tip of the island (tel: 78.53.92). Open: daily. Admission charge.

POINTE DU BOUT AND LES TROIS-ILETS

A 20-minute ferry ride from Fort-de-France, Pointe du Bout is the site of most of the island's luxury hotels, a few trendy boutiques and a yacht-filled marina. Near by, Les Trois-Ilets, one of Martinique's prettiest villages, was once one of the most prosperous towns on the island with nine refineries working the local sugar plantations.

Southwest of Fort-de-France. Ferries run regularly from Fort-de-France esplanade.

St-Pierre and its bay

ROCHER DU DIAMANT (DIAMOND ROCK)

A large rock can be spotted just off shore between Les Anses-d'Arlets and Le Diamant. Remarkably, this uninspiring piece of real estate was commissioned as a sloop of war, named HMS *Diamond Rock*, by the British navy. They manned it with a garrison of 120 in 1804 and held it in the face of heavy French bombardment for 18 months. The siege was eventually broken, so the story goes, when the French floated over several barrels of rum which were taken on board by the thirsty defenders. Now the island is home to thousands of seabirds.

Palace of culture

ST-PIERRE

Once considered the Paris of the West Indies, St-Pierre was completely devastated at 8am on 8 May 1902 when Mount Pelée erupted. Within three minutes a huge avalanche of ash and cinders and poisonous fumes had wiped out all but one of its population of more than 30,000. The sole survivor was a prisoner named Cyparis, held in an underground jail cell. Today it is Martinique's version of Pompeii; statues lie where they were toppled, once fashionable boulevards have vanished beneath a tangle of tropical growth. Twelve ships were also destroyed at the time of the eruption and lie at the bottom of St-Pierre Bay. Because bones of seamen were found on board the bay is treated as a memorial grave and protected. There is a museum documenting the disaster in the middle of the village and a small motorised train, called the Cyparis Express, offers guided tours of the historic town.

On the west coast, approximately 15km north of Fort-de-France. Museum (tel: 78 15 16). Open: daily, 9am–noon and 3pm–6pm. Admission charge. *(See also page 84.)*

SOUTHERN AREAS

The southern quarter of Martinique is known for its gentle scenery, pretty fishing villages and beautiful beaches.

Rivière-Pilote

An agricultural town with, near by, a large 'pitt' where traditional cock fights are held, as well as fights between mongoose and snakes. The mongoose and the snake are put into a glass case, bets are laid and usually the mongoose comes up trumps.

Near Rivière-Pilote, **Le Mauny**

Pleasurecraft for hire at Grande Anse des Salines

Distillery makes one of the best-known rums on the island; visitors are welcome and there is a chance to taste the product.
Le Mauny Distillery has guided tours five times daily (except Sundays) at 10am, 11am, 12.30pm, 2pm, and 3pm.

Sainte-Anne
Sainte-Anne is one of Martinique's most charming villages. Certainly its beach is the best and very popular. Fortunately the centre is separated from its strip of sand, so it remains peaceful even when the beach is busy. There is a fine old sandstone parish church, dating back to 1824, and a small market by the waterfront – but mostly Sainte-Anne is given over to providing for the tourist with good hotels and restaurants. South of Sainte-Anne, at **Grande Anse des Salines**, is one of the best and therefore busiest beaches on the island. Near by at **La Savane** is a petrified forest.

Sainte-Luce
An important fishing centre whose beach is very popular with tourists, Ste-Luce is a peaceful village (but, this being a part of France, it is a peaceful village with a good pâtisserie). A hike inland leads the visitor to the **Montravail Forest**, where there are picnic facilities and a superb viewpoint overlooking the island of St Lucia.

KNOTS
According to tradition the Madras headscarf as worn by the Martiniquais women holds a hidden message. The code is in the knots on top: One knot means the lady's heart is free, two knots means her heart is engaged (but you can try), three knots means her heart is engaged (full stop), four knots means everyone who tries is welcome.

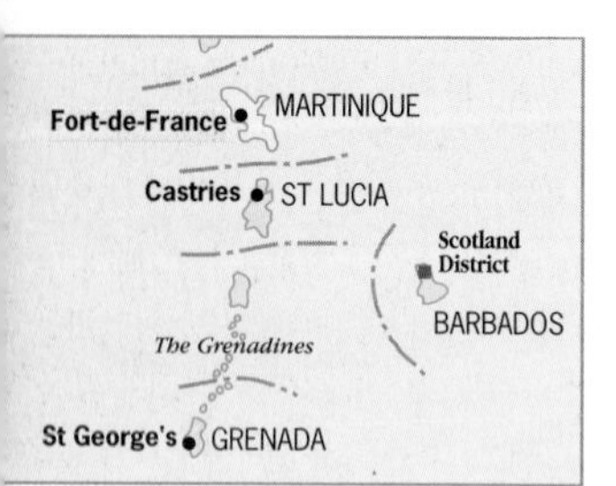

Martinique Drive

A journey by car through some of the most fertile areas north of Fort-de-France to the ruins of St-Pierre, the town devastated by a volcanic eruption. For the drive route, see the main Martinique map on page 79. ***Allow about 5 hours.***

Leave Fort-de-France on the Morne Rouge road at the old cemetery where it begins to climb through an avenue of breadfruit, avocado, mango and coconut trees. A lush valley of sugar cane appears to the right, while behind the view extends across the Lamentin Plain. Follow the signs for Balata Church.

1 SACRE-COEUR

Rather incongrously set in a tropical landscape, this is a miniature copy, in pink, of the Sacré-Coeur in Paris.
Carry on along the road to the sign to Balata Gardens.

2 BALATA TROPICAL BOTANICAL PARK

This privately run park in the shadow of the Pitons is a collection of both common-or-garden and rare tropical plants built up over 20 years. All of Martinique's most beautiful flowers can be seen here in carefully laid-out gardens – heliconia, begonias, orchids, water-lillies – as well as some true curiosities. A restored Creole house has period furnishings and prints illustrating early plantation life.

3 LA ROUTE DE LA TRACE

Known simply as la Trace, this is the central highland road which winds past the Pitons du Carbet through the rainforest to the foot of Mount Pelée.

Tucked into paradise: Anse Turin's miniscule Gauguin Museum

The highest point is a village called Dans les Nuages. There is a pleasant place to stop for a picnic by the Alma River, once the road has started to descend. Beyond this there is a marked trail up to the top of Piton Boucher.

At Le Morne Rouge, turn left towards St-Pierre.

4 MONTAGNE PELEE

The cause of St-Pierre's demise, Mount Pelée (1,397m) is clearly visible to the right. As soon as you enter St-Pierre you see the ruins of buildings destroyed by the eruption.

5 ST-PIERRE

The first stop in this now quiet fishing village should be at the museum overlooking the bay founded by American volcanologist Frank Perret. Exhibits recall the glorious days of 'the Paris of the West Indies' and tell the stories of what happened at 8am on 8 May 1902. A number of clocks are on display, stopped at the moment the city was engulfed. Further along Rue Victor Hugo is the old prison in which Cyparis survived.

Continue south along the coast.

6 ANSE TURIN

A short distance inland from the beach, La Vallée des Papillons is a botanical garden set among the ruins of a 17th-century settlement. You tour the grounds in a cloud of butterflies. A little further on along the main road is the tiny Paul Gauguin Museum. The painter lived near here for five months in 1887, a short but important period of his life, and there are reproductions of about 20 works from his Martinique period on display.

From here it is a leisurely drive down the coast through the villages of Bellefontaine, Case-Pilote and Schoelcher back to Fort-de-France.

Not Paris, but Martinique: a pink, Caribbean Sacré-Coeur

Balata Park (tel: 72 58 82). Open: daily, 9am–6pm. The Volcano Museum (tel: 78 15 16). Open: daily, 9am–noon and 3pm–5pm. Vallée des Papillons: Open: daily, 9am–5pm. Paul Gauguin Museum (tel: 77 22 66). Open: daily, 10am–5pm. Admission charged at them all.

MUSIC

There is music just about everywhere in the Caribbean. Taxis cruise the streets with speakers blaring; shops crank up the volume to draw in business; an impromptu band gets together on the back of a truck to serenade the Saturday market; often, at night, huge banks of speakers are set up in the middle of a village or at the side of the road for no better reason than a sort of collective joie de vivre.

There are several different styles of island sounds. **Calypso** is rooted in the old days of slavery and sugar plantations. Music gave the slaves a means of protest and calypso today is still a powerful mixture of music and message, although now the protest tends to be about modern social ills or unpopular politicians. However, it has its lighter side and a talented calypsonian can provoke gales of laughter from his audience. Traditionally accompanied by a band of steel drums known as pans, which have been punched and hammered and tempered to produce a range of notes, calypso often makes one of the enduring memories of a Caribbean holiday.

A more modern style of music mixes calypso with soul and is called **soca**. It evolved in the 1970s when American music dominated the islands' airwaves and is often played at island parties. On the French islands, the thrilling double beat of **zouk** music is descended from the old island rhythms of the beguine.

Although **reggae** comes from Jamaica, its infectious rhythms are heard on all the eastern islands as well. It particularly appeals to members of the younger generation, who play the

protest songs loudly on their portable music systems. At Christmas, Trinidad and Tobago light up with the sound of **parang** music drawn from South America.

However, the oldest sounds to be heard in the Caribbean are likely to emanate from the fungi or **scratch bands** of the Virgin Islands. These follow the slave tradition of making music with whatever is at hand. It is not unusual to see someone shaking a bean-filled gourd or rattling a washboard in the search for that certain island rhythm.

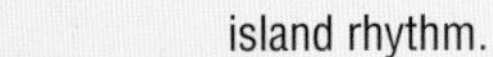

Top left: calypso player
Far left: steel band in action on Tobago
Left: making steel drums on Trinidad
Above: learning the drums
Top: doin' it nice!

St Lucia

St Lucia is the largest of the English-speaking Windward Islands and a nature lover's delight. Its dramatic topography includes lush volcanic mountains, natural hot springs, valleys covered in tropical fruit and flowers, and soft sandy beaches.

The first European to settle on St Lucia was Francois de Clerc, a pirate also known as Jambe de Bois or Wooden Leg, who established his base at Pigeon Island and regularly set out from there to attack passing ships. During the years of disputes which followed over who actually owned the island, St Lucia changed hands 14 times before finally being ceded to the British in 1814. Even today, however, the Creole patois displays much French influence. St Lucia achieved independence on 22 February 1979.

CASTRIES

Castries is one of the 'newest' cities in the Caribbean, thanks to a run of disastrous fires between 1796 and 1948 which meant most of it had to be rebuilt. Fortunately there are still a few of the older buildings left standing, with their graceful balconies and intricate latticework intact.

Stylish painting of the island's national bird, the endangered St Lucia parrot

Castries Cathedral

On the east side of the square, the Cathedral of the Immaculate Conception is one of the largest churches in the eastern Caribbean. It was built in 1897 and became a cathedral in 1957 when the Castries diocese was established. Although it seems sombre and grey on the outside, inside it reveals a delicate, more colourful image. The murals are by the St Lucian artist Dunstan St Omer.

Central Market

Saturday morning is the best time to come to this colourful market when farmers from the villages, who cannot get a place inside, spread out their produce in front of its bright red façade. It was built by engineers from Liverpool in England in 1894 and, despite all the natural disasters which have befallen the city since then, the market has remained virtually untouched. Apart from fruit and vegetables, islanders also sell traditional clay pots, baskets and 'market' dolls.

Jeremie Street. Open: Monday to Saturday, 6am–5pm.

ST LUCIA

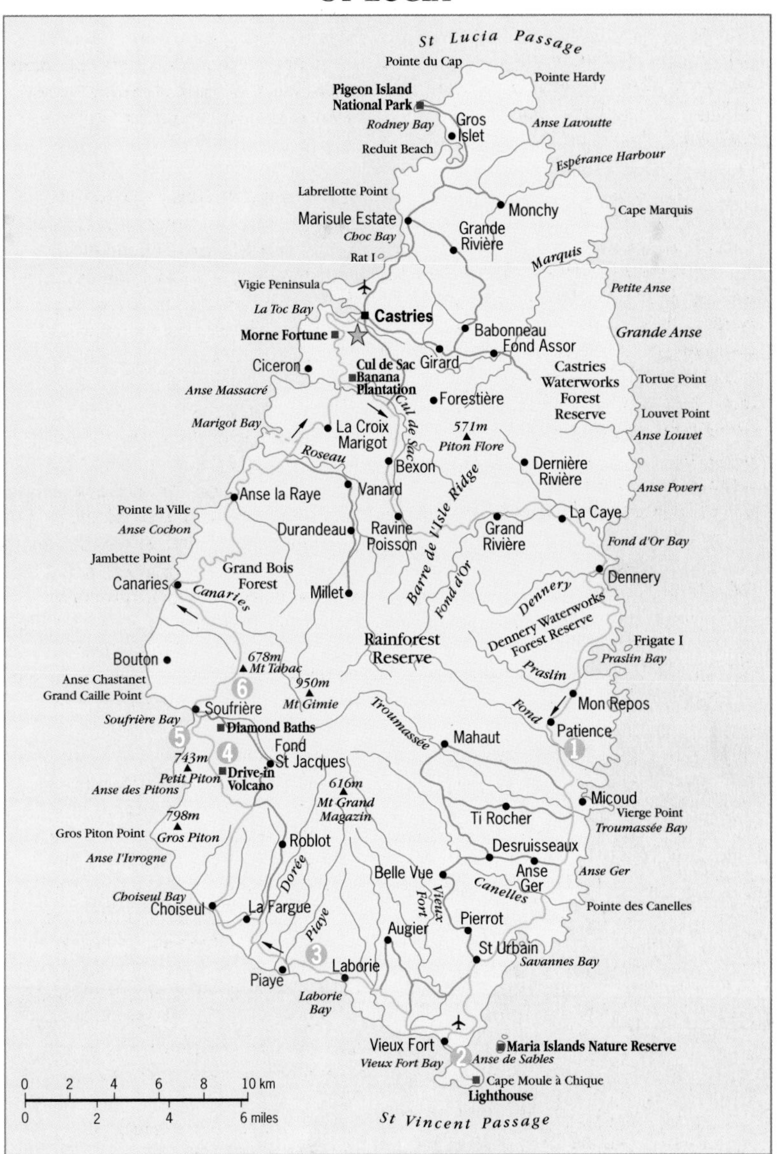
St Lucia Passage
Pointe du Cap
Pointe Hardy
Pigeon Island National Park
Rodney Bay
Gros Islet
Anse Lavoutte
Reduit Beach
Espérance Harbour
Labrellotte Point
Monchy
Marisule Estate
Cape Marquis
Grande Rivière
Choc Bay
Rat I
Marquis
Vigie Peninsula
Petite Anse
La Toc Bay
Castries
Morne Fortune
Babonneau
Grande Anse
Fond Assor
Girard
Ciceron
Cul de Sac Banana Plantation
Castries Waterworks Forest Reserve
Tortue Point
Anse Massacré
Forestière
Louvet Point
Marigot Bay
La Croix Marigot
Cul de Sac
571m
Piton Flore
Anse Louvet
Roseau
Bexon
Dernière Rivière
Vanard
Anse Povert
Anse la Raye
Pointe la Ville
Barre de l'Isle Ridge
La Caye
Anse Cochon
Durandeau
Ravine Poisson
Grand Rivière
Fond d'Or Bay
Jambette Point
Grand Bois Forest
Dennery
Canaries
Millet
Fond d'Or
Dennery
Canaries
Dennery Waterworks Forest Reserve
Frigate I
Rainforest Reserve
Praslin Bay
Bouton
678m
Mt Tabac
Praslin
Anse Chastanet
950m
Grand Caille Point
Mt Gimie
Fond
Mon Repos
Soufrière
Troumassée
Patience
Soufrière Bay
Diamond Baths
Mahaut
Fond St Jacques
743m
Drive-in Volcano
Petit Piton
616m
Micoud
Anse des Pitons
Mt Grand Magazin
Vierge Point
798m
Ti Rocher
Troumassée Bay
Gros Piton Point
Gros Piton
Roblot
Desruisseaux
Anse l'Ivrogne
Dorée
Belle Vue
Anse Ger
Anse Ger
Vieux Fort
Canelles
Choiseul Bay
Choiseul
La Fargue
Pointe des Canelles
Piaye
Augier
Pierrot
St Urbain
Savannes Bay
Laborie
Piaye
Laborie Bay
Vieux Fort
Maria Islands Nature Reserve
Anse de Sables
Vieux Fort Bay
Cape Moule à Chique Lighthouse
0 2 4 6 8 10 km
0 2 4 6 miles
St Vincent Passage

Columbus Square
The centre of the town is its most peaceful spot, Columbus Square, a small park known as the Place d'Armes to the French. There is a bandstand, a memorial to the dead of the two World Wars and a remarkably venerable saman tree. Some people think it may be as much as 400 years old, others trace it back merely to the French Revolution of 1789. Its local name has been the Massav Tree since a visitor asked a taxi driver what it was. He replied *Massav* – which actually means 'I don't know' in patois, but the visitor thought that was its name.

Fort Charlotte
The best preserved of the many fortifications on Morne Fortune, this fort on the summit of the hill was begun as the 'Citadelle du Morne Fortune' by the French in 1764 (the section built in stone) and completed as Fort Charlotte 30 years later by the British (the red-brick section). Many of the original buildings, the gun emplacements and the cannons are still in place and the barracks and the guard rooms have been restored for use as an educational centre by the St Lucia National Trust.
Morne Fortune. Open access. National Trust (tel: 452 5005).

Market hall overspill: traders and browsers in the open in Castries

Government House
There are spectacular views of Castries from Morne Fortune, the road which snakes up the hill to the south of the city. Government House is also the official residence of the Governor-General. An outstanding example of Victorian colonial architecture, it stands on the site of some of the fiercest battles between French and British forces in the 18th and 19th centuries. The most famous took place on 24 May 1796, when the Royal Inniskilling Fusiliers captured the area after a long and vicious struggle. A monument to the battle still stands today.
Morne Fortune. Not open, but ask the guard for permission to photograph the house.

JUMP UP
During the rest of the week it seems a mild-mannered sort of place, but every Friday night the fishing village of Gros Islet in the north of the island comes alive with a huge street party. Large speakers are wheeled out on to the road, everyone dances in the streets, food vendors sell local specialities. It's good clean fun – most of the time. Plan to arrive from 9pm onwards.
8km along the main road north of Castries.

One for the chop: coconut seller, Castries market

CENTRAL RAINFOREST RESERVE

More than 10 per cent of St Lucia is covered by rainforest and many visitors – ready to take a break from sunning themselves on the island's beaches – welcome the opportunity to explore its inland scenery. The Central Rainforest Reserve is part of the Central Highlands. An 11km trail links the villages of Mahaut on the east and Fond St Jacques to the west. From its highest point there are superb views of the rest of the Central Highlands, the Pitons and Mount Gimie, the highest peak on the island. Regular hikes are run by the Forestry Department, or visitors may follow the trail themselves, provided they secure permission from the department beforehand.

In the centre of the island. The trail is easily reached from both the main west coast or the east coast roads. St Lucia Forestry Department (tel: 450 2231).

FRIGATE ISLANDS

The two Frigate Islands lie just off the east coast of St Lucia. Together they draw ornithologists eager to watch the nesting and roosting of colonies of frigates, particularly during May and June when flocks of them seem to hang above the islands like a cloud. Permission is required from the St Lucia National Trust to visit the islands, but there is a nature trail on the mainland which leads through dense vegetation, across the cliffs and to a lookout opposite the islands.

Nature trail: between the villages of Micoud and Dennery on the east coast road.

Marigot Bay manages to keep its character despite being a stop-off for charter yachts

MARIA ISLANDS

The Maria Islands Nature Reserve, consisting of Maria Major and Maria Minor, offer a protected environment for many rare species of wildlife, including several not known to exist elsewhere in the Caribbean. Here one finds the harmless Couresse grass snake, considered the rarest snake in the world, and the colourful Maria Islands ground lizard. The region is also a nesting site for seabirds and turtles.

Off the east coast road by Vieux Fort. While the reserve is closed during the nesting season, tours can be arranged through the Maria Islands Interpretation Centre (tel: 24094).

MARIGOT BAY

A winding road leading from Cul de Sac Valley drops down to one of the prettiest natural harbours on the island. Framed on three sides by steep green hills, the bay is skirted by coconut palms and is a tranquil, idyllic place, although there has been much development here in recent years to provide moorings for charter yachts. Besides its scenic attractions, Marigot Bay is also remembered by some people of a certain age as the place where Dr Dolittle was given a lift inside the shell of the giant pink snail in the film *Dr Dolittle*.

PIGEON ISLAND NATIONAL PARK

Named because Admiral Rodney reputedly kept pigeons, this 16 hectare island has been an Arawak settlement and a Carib stronghold, a haven for pirates who preyed on passing ships, a strategic British fort, a quarantine station, a whaling station, and a United States naval station. Now it is a protected national park. Connected to the mainland by a man-made causeway, it has organised trails leading to the promontory known as Pigeon Point. Here there are the ruins of Fort Rodney, from where the famous admiral kept an eye on the French fleet across in Martinique before he led his forces to defeat Admiral Grasse at the Battle of the Saintes in 1782.

The park is located at the northern tip of the island. The Pigeon Point Museum: Open: Monday to Saturday, 9am–4pm. Admission charge.

THE PITONS

The twin peaks of Petit Piton (743m) and Gros Piton (798m) dominate the southwestern corner of the island, not to mention every guidebook and poster of St Lucia. They are thought to be the result of an eruption which occurred 15,000 years ago. They can be climbed and guides are available, but the route is rated as difficult even by experienced mountaineers.

(For a closer look at the Pitons, the village

of Soufrière and Diamond Baths see the **St Lucia Drive**, page 94.)

ST LUCIA'S BEACHES

All St Lucia's beaches are public but few have changing facilities or toilets. **Reduit Beach** is one of the most popular strips of sand, with several top hotels near by. **Choc Bay** is popular with local families at weekends. **Anse des Pitons** has the most spectacular setting on the island. **Anse Cochon** is one of the most secluded. **Cas En Bas** is usually good for wind-surfing, while **Anse Chastanet**, north of Soufrière, has some of the best snorkelling around, particularly in the area known as the Key Hole Pinnacles. A map detailing all these beaches is available from the local tourist office.

VIGIE PENINSULA

Another witness to the struggle between France and Britain, Vigie Peninsula to the north of Castries was the sight of two famous battles, both of which went in favour of the British; on Rat Island, opposite the peninsula, are the remnants of some British barracks. Dominated by its lighthouse, Vigie Point (French for look-out) is now home to several diplomatic missions as well as the offices of the St Lucia Archaeological and Historical Society and the National Trust.

A short distance north of Castries and in close proximity to Vigie airport.

Dramatic scenery at Soufrière, including one of the Pitons

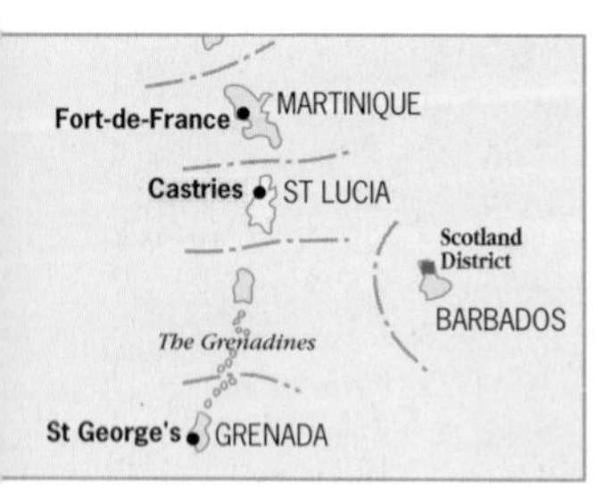

St Lucia Drive

This excursion concentrates on the spectacular scenery in the south. The east coast road still needs care in parts to avoid potholes but the west coast road was being rebuilt when this book went to press. Take your swimming costume. For the route, see the St Lucia map on page 89. *Allow a full day.*

Leave Castries by the southern Morne Fortune road. Pause to admire the view of the town, its harbour, Vigie Peninsula and the northern coast of the island from the new lookout on the left-hand side of the road.

After the road descends to the south take the left fork at the Cul de Sac banana plantation and cross the island over the Barre de l'Isle, its mountainous spine.

1 THE EAST COAST

This road, which passes through the villages of Dennery and Micoud, hugs the Atlantic coast of the island. In many parts dramatic rock formations have been created by the pounding seas, while elsewhere there are deep bays with protected anchorages.

At Praslin Bay look out for men making traditional dug-out boats from gommier trees.

The Maria Islands appear as the east coast road turns towards Vieux Fort.

2 VIEUX FORT

One of the island's original settlements, Vieux Fort is now an industrial centre and the site of the international airport. However, there are beaches here which are good for picnicking and a short detour can be made along the Moule à Chique peninsula to reach the lighthouse.

Continue along the main road.

The bleached, corrugated-iron rooftops of Canaries, on the west coast of the island

Pulling a boat ashore at Choiseul, south coast

3 LABORIE AND CHOISEUL

Laborie is a picturesque fishing village of wooden colonial buildings. Choiseul is considered the craft centre of the island and many villagers work at home carving wood, throwing pots and weaving baskets. As you leave the village note the Amerindian petroglyphs (rock-carvings) on the large rock beside the road.

4 THE DRIVE-IN VOLCANO

Close to the Pitons, southeast of Soufrière, is a 3 hectare crater often referred to as a drive-in volcano. The road does indeed lead into an area of coloured earth and rocks and pools of boiling mud. A walk through the crater leads past more than a dozen of these pools and hot springs. A guide is not usually needed, but watch where you put your feet.

Follow the signs to the Diamond Baths.

5 DIAMOND BATHS

The Diamond Botanical Gardens and Mineral Baths were built in 1785 for the soldiers of Louis XVI. The baths were almost totally destroyed during the French Revolution but have recently been restored and for a small fee visitors can enjoy a natural hot bath after a tour of the grounds and botanical gardens.

Return to the main road and drive to Soufrière.

6 SOUFRIERE

This fishing port has a spectacular setting. The town is St Lucia's oldest and under the French was an important trade centre. The main square has good examples of French colonial architecture.

From Soufrière, the road runs through a spectacular wild garden of fruit trees and flowers to the peaceful towns of Canaries and Anse la Raye, then down to the Roseau banana plantation.

Here there is an optional detour to beautiful Marigot Bay. Return on the main road to Castries.

The Diamond Baths. Open: daily, 10am–5pm. Admission charge.
Drive-in Volcano. Open: daily, 9am–5pm. Admission charge.

Barbados

Barbados, perhaps the most 'British' of all the islands, knows how to appeal to its visitors and to entice them back; here there are first-class hotels, excellent restaurants, beautiful beaches, sports – in and out of the water – of all descriptions; there is scenery to admire, wildlife to photograph and history to explore. In short, Barbados has something for everyone.

BRIDGETOWN

Founded in 1628, the capital of the island is named after an old Amerindian bridge which once spanned the Careenage, the city's central waterway. Most of the island's 250,000 population live here.

Bridgetown Synagogue

One of the oldest synagogues this side of the Atlantic, originally constructed in 1656 by Jews from Brazil and renovated in 1833 after hurricane damage. However, many of the tombstones still date back to the 17th century and the internal structure has been stripped back to the original roof timbers and coral stone.
Magazine Lane. Open: Monday to Friday, 9am–4pm.

St Michael's Cathedral

St Michael's Cathedral, rebuilt in 1789, stands on the site of the original 1665 church. At one time its arched roof was the widest in the world.
St Michael's Row. Open access.

Trafalgar Square

On the north bank of the Careenage stands Bridgetown's best-known landmark, **Nelson's statue** in Trafalgar Square. The work of Sir Richard Westmacott, it was raised in 1813 and predates the column in London by 36 years. To the north of the square, a group of neo-Gothic buildings houses the **Barbados Parliament**, the third oldest in the English-speaking world. The stained-glass windows feature British monarchs from King James I to Queen Victoria.
Parliament Buildings: (Government Information Service tel: 427 6220). Opening times vary.

ANDROMEDA GARDENS

Acquired by the National Trust in the late 1980s from a private owner, this beautiful garden, incorporating a stream and landscaped waterfalls, is internationally renowned for the variety and quality of its tropical blooms. There are separate sections for orchids, palms, heliconia, hibiscus, cacti and succulents and, in more shady places, ferns, aroids and begonias. The gardens are particularly interesting to professional botanists and horticulturalists, for the founder's hobby involved testing species, acquired mostly by exchange from botanical gardens around the world, to see how they would fare in Barbados' climate.
Location: near Bathsheba on the east coast (tel: 433 9261). Open: daily, 8am–sunset. Admission charge.

ANIMAL FLOWER CAVE

This cave at the north of the island comprises a series of caverns formed by the sea and is famous for its abundance of colourful sea anemones. Children in particular enjoy watching them open and

Bridgetown centre from the Careenage

close their flower-like tendrils. Care needs to be taken when scrambling on the rocks.
Off Highway 1, at the top, most northerly point of the island (tel: 439 8797). The cave can be safely approached from land by a series of steps. Open: daily, 9am–5pm. Admission charge.

BARBADOS MUSEUM
Formerly a military prison, the museum houses an extensive collection of Amerindian artefacts tracing the Arawak and Carib routes through the Caribbean, together with mementoes from the days of sugar and slavery. There is also an exhibition concerned with the country's fauna and flora, as well as a good collection of old maps and photographs, and a reconstructed prisoner's cell. The complex includes a library and shops, and its café provides the setting for a weekend evening entertainment of feasting and light history called '1627 and All That'.
Garrison Savannah (tel: 427 0201). Open: Monday to Saturday, 9am–6pm. Admission charge.

BATHSHEBA
Bathsheba is a quiet fishing village made famous by its setting close to the 305m limestone walls of Hackleton's Cliff, overlooking Tent Bay. At the beginning of the century it was a favourite holiday spot reached by a now-defunct railway line from Bridgetown. The Atlantis Hotel in the centre of the village is known the world over for its Bajan Sunday lunches, while the Bathsheba Soup Bowl, so-called for the effect of the waves in the bay, is the setting for international surfing competitions.
On the east coast of the island.

NELSON

Nelson in Bridgetown

BARBADOS

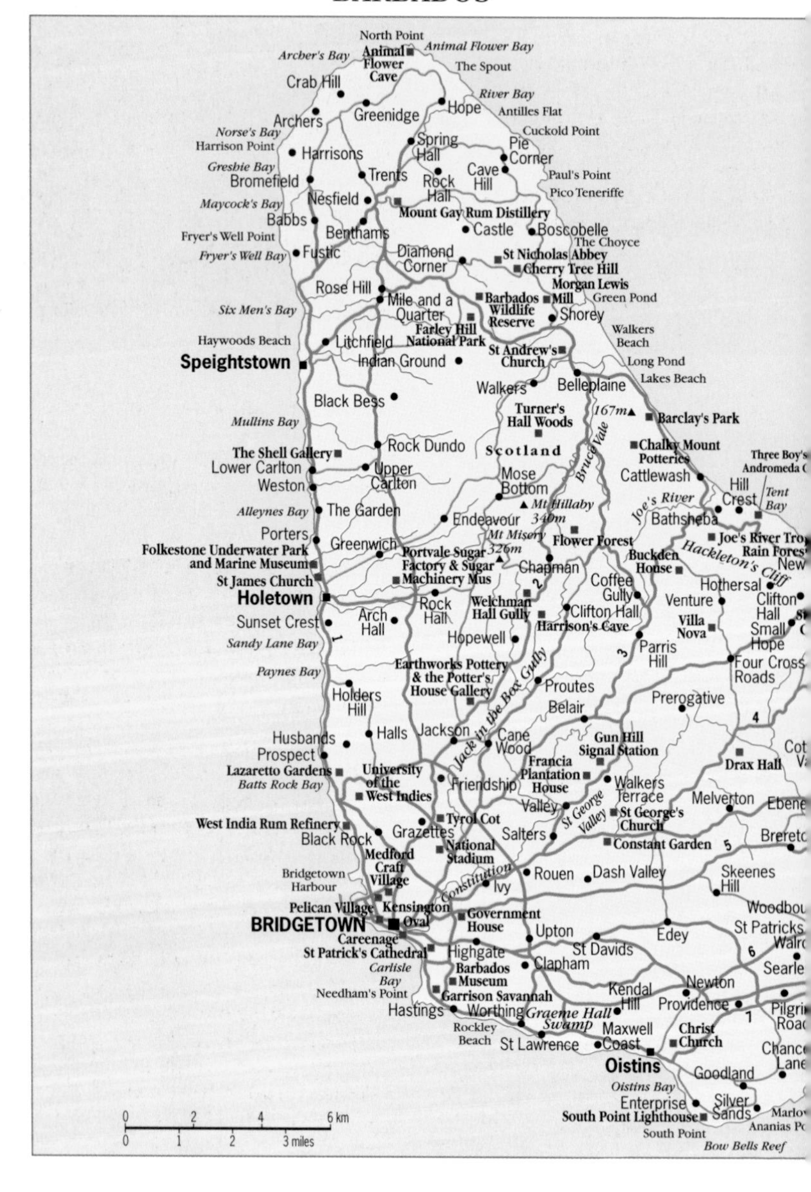
North Point
Animal Flower Cave
Animal Flower Bay
Archer's Bay
The Spout
Crab Hill
River Bay
Archers
Greenidge
Hope
Antilles Flat
Norse's Bay
Harrison Point
Cuckold Point
Spring Hall
Pie Corner
Harrisons
Greshie Bay
Bromefield
Trents
Rock Hall
Cave Hill
Paul's Point
Pico Teneriffe
Maycock's Bay
Nesfield
Mount Gay Rum Distillery
Babbs
Benthams
Castle
Boscobelle
Fryer's Well Point
The Choyce
Fryer's Well Bay
Fustic
Diamond Corner
St Nicholas Abbey
Cherry Tree Hill
Morgan Lewis Mill
Rose Hill
Mile and a Quarter
Barbados Wildlife Reserve
Green Pond
Six Men's Bay
Shorey
Farley Hill National Park
Walkers Beach
Haywoods Beach
Litchfield
St Andrew's Church
Speightstown
Indian Ground
Long Pond
Lakes Beach
Belleplaine
Walkers
Black Bess
Turner's Hall Woods
167m
Barclay's Park
Mullins Bay
Rock Dundo
Chalky Mount Potteries
The Shell Gallery
Scotland
Bruce Vale
Three Boy's
Andromeda
Lower Carlton
Upper Carlton
Mose Bottom
Cattlewash
Weston
Hill Crest
Tent Bay
Alleynes Bay
The Garden
Mt Hillaby 340m
Joe's River
Bathsheba
Endeavour
Porters
Mt Misery 326m
Flower Forest
Joe's River Tro
Rain Fores
Folkestone Underwater Park and Marine Museum
Greenwich
Portvale Sugar Factory & Sugar Machinery Mus
Chapman
Buckden House
Hackleton's Cliff
New
St James Church
Coffee Gully
Hothersal
Holetown
Welchman Hall Gully
Clifton Hall
Venture
Clifton Hall
Rock Hall
Arch Hall
Harrison's Cave
Villa Nova
Sunset Crest
Small Hope
Sandy Lane Bay
Hopewell
Parris Hill
Four Cross Roads
Earthworks Pottery & the Potter's House Gallery
Paynes Bay
Jack in the Box Gully
Proutes
Holders Hill
Prerogative
Belair
Husbands
Halls
Jackson
Cane Wood
Gun Hill Signal Station
Prospect
Drax Hall
Lazaretto Gardens
University of the West Indies
Francia Plantation House
Batts Rock Bay
Friendship
Walkers Terrace
Melverton
Valley
St George Valley
West India Rum Refinery
Tyrol Cot
St George's Church
Black Rock
Grazettes
Salters
Constant Garden
Medford Craft Village
National Stadium
Bridgetown Harbour
Rouen
Dash Valley
Skeenes Hill
Constitution
Ivy
Pelican Village
Kensington Oval
Government House
BRIDGETOWN
Upton
Edey
St Patricks
Careenage
St Patrick's Cathedral
Highgate
St Davids
Carlisle Bay
Barbados Museum
Clapham
Searle
Needham's Point
Garrison Savannah
Kendal Hill
Newton
Providence
Hastings
Worthing
Graeme Hall Swamp
Rockley Beach
St Lawrence
Maxwell Coast
Christ Church
Oistins
Goodland
Oistins Bay
Enterprise
Silver Sands
South Point Lighthouse
South Point
Bow Bells Reef
0 2 4 6 km
0 1 2 3 miles

CODRINGTON COLLEGE

One of the island's most interesting buildings, Codrington College was founded in the 17th century by Christopher Codrington, a wealthy planter who became, at the age of 30, Governor of the Leeward Islands. The building was founded under his will of 1702 and was finally opened in 1745 as a theological college for the Anglican priesthood. Note in particular the magnificent avenue of royal palms and the impressive façade. There is also a large lily pond (the flowers close during the day).

Near the eastern tip of the island. Although visitors may tour the grounds it is not usually possible to go inside.

Barbados boats

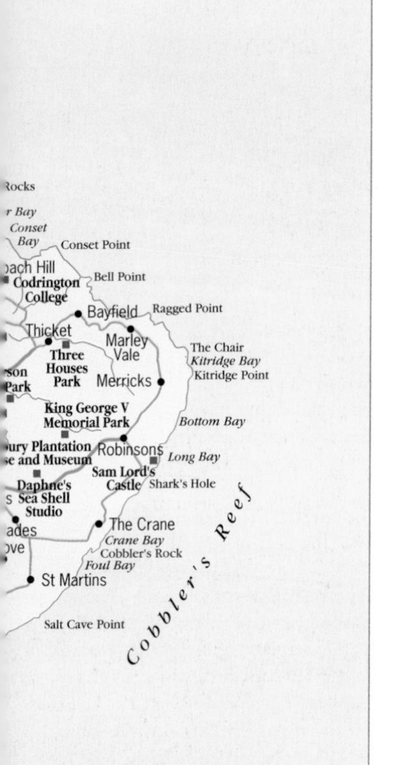

FRANCIA PLANTATION HOUSE

Situated on a wooded hillside above the St George Valley, Francia is a well-maintained greathouse (as the plantation owners' grand houses were called) from the beginning of the century. The walls

HERITAGE PASSPORT

An economical way to see the sights of Barbados is to purchase a Heritage Passport, a pass which gives reduced admission to 11 National Trust properties around the island including Welchman Hall Gully, Gun Hill Signal Station and the Andromeda Botanical Gardens. It is available from the Barbados tourist office and its representatives around the world, or from Ronald Tree House, 10th Avenue, Belleville, 87 Michael, Barbados (tel: 436 9033).

Plantation splendour at Francia

inside are hung with part of the owner's extensive collection of antique maps and prints, including one of the earliest maps of the Caribbean dating from 1522. The watercolours of Gun Hill Signal Station were painted by Lionel Grimstone Fox in 1879. Francia is still owned and occupied by the descendants of the original owner. *Between St George's Parish Church and Gun Hill Station, about 8km from Bridgetown (tel: 429 0474). Open: Monday to Friday, 10am–4pm. Admission charge.*

GARRISON SAVANNAH

Dating from the 17th century, this was once considered the finest parade ground in the Caribbean. Now the island's main race track, it is still used for its original purpose once a year on Independence Day. Surrounding the Savannah are several historical buildings including the Savannah Club and the old Drill Hall. Behind the Savannah are the ruins of Fort Charles and St Anne's Fort, part of the British defences begun in 1649. *3km south of central Bridgetown.*

GUN HILL SIGNAL STATION

This was part of a chain of signal stations built in 1818 and provides a good view over the south of the island. Originally intended to give an early warning of invasion and to report the safe arrival of cargo ships, it was restored by the National Trust in 1982 and contains an interesting collection of military memorabilia. Beneath the station is a coral-stone lion carved in 1868, thought

to be symbolic of the British Empire.
On Highway 4 from Bridgetown. Open: daily, 9am–5pm. Admission charge.

HARRISON'S CAVE
This is actually a series of caverns complete with stalactites and stalagmites. Close to the cave's lowest point, a 12m waterfall drops into a dark green lake. A tram takes visitors into the chambers.
In the centre of the island, off Highway 2 (tel: 438 6640). Open: daily, 9am–4pm. Admission charge.

SOUTH POINT LIGHTHOUSE
This unique iron lighthouse was made in England and exhibited in 1851 at the Great Exhibition in London before being dismantled and shipped to Barbados.
Close to the village of Oistins in the south.

VILLA NOVA
A superbly preserved greathouse built of Barbadian coral stone in 1834 by Edmund Haynes, a successful sugar baron and owner of a 400 hectare estate. Set in an ornate tropical garden, the mansion's subsequent owners have included Sir Anthony Eden, the former British prime minister. The two portlandia trees in the garden were planted by Queen Elizabeth II in 1966.
In St John's parish on the east of the island (tel: 433 1524). Open: Monday to Friday, 9am–4pm. Admission charge.

WELCHMAN HALL GULLY
A 1km ravine in the coral limestone near Harrison's Cave is now a nature reserve and one of the island's top attractions. It was converted into a tropical fruit and spice garden in the mid-18th century and then abandoned and left to grow wild for over 50 years, until the National Trust purchased the whole area. Some flowering plants were added, but the Trust left much of the gully in its natural state. A 800m long path meanders through the reserve, thick with dark green vegetation, under the shade of palms and exotic ferns. There might be a glimpse of one of the wild green African monkeys which live in the area. The gully also has some interesting geological phenomena, including a massive pillar, supporting a cliff, which was created by the union of a stalactite and a stalagmite centuries ago.
In the centre of the island off Highway 2. Open: daily, 9am–5pm. Admission charge.

Immaculate shops at St Lawrence, in the far south of the island

THE GREEN FLASH
There is a moment, just when the last rays of the sun dip below the sea when, if you are really lucky, it is possible to see a clear green flash on the horizon. It is rare, but it happens, and avid sunset watchers will travel far on a clear evening in the hope of seeing it. The west coast beaches of Barbados are particularly recommended. (A couple of rum punches helps as well.)

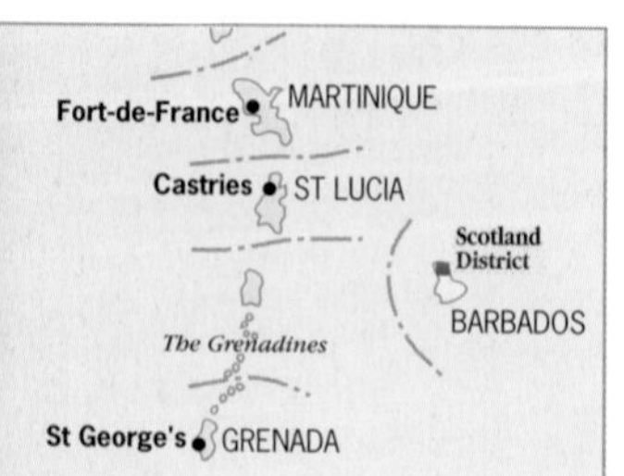

Barbados Walk

This walk includes some of the most interesting sites in the north of Barbados. It is best to set off early before the day has got too hot as there are some steep climbs. Take some cold drinks or perhaps a picnic for Farley Hill. *Allow about 3 hours.*

Follow Highway 2 up Farley Hill in the St Peter district and take the last turn on the left before Farley Hill Park. Park near Bleak House; it is a private dwelling so it is important not to park in the drive.

1 BLEAK HOUSE

Built originally in 1860 after years of litigation between two families, and named after the Dickens' novel which deals with interminable wrangles over property, the house was bought in 1983 as a burnt-out shell and has been rebuilt by the current owner in a classic Georgian style. Take the path to the left of the house near the entrance, past the pig farm and leading down the hill. On a clear day there are superb views of the whole of the St Andrews district. Notice the ridge of hills to the south with their profile said to resemble the sleeping Nelson.

Walk back to Highway 2, turn left towards Farley Hill and just before it take the path to your right. Keeping left at all forks, follow

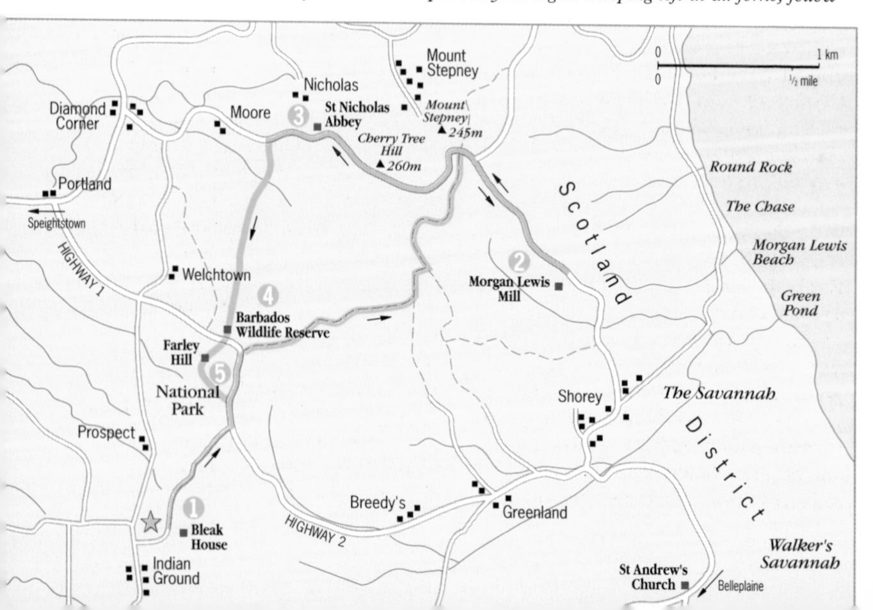

the path to reach the road near Mount Stepney. Turn right here and follow the road downhill to reach Morgan Lewis Mill.

2 MORGAN LEWIS MILL

The only remaining intact sugar mill of the 300 which once worked on the island was built in the 17th century. The mill has been restored by the National Trust, and its wheelhouse and sails are in perfect order.

Retrace your steps up the steep road to Cherry Tree Hill, an impressive 550m avenue of mahogany trees. Keep on the road to reach St Nicholas Abbey.

3 ST NICHOLAS ABBEY

The oldest of the island's many historic houses, St Nicholas Abbey was built some time between 1650 and 1660, with curved gables in the Jacobean style. It is one of only three such plantation houses of that period in the western hemisphere. Inside is an impressive collection of 18th-century furniture, a Coalport dinner service and Wedgwood miniatures. The current owner shows visitors a remarkably preserved home movie of early 20th-century plantation life.

Continue ahead on the road and after a short while take the path on the left. Ask for directions for the short cut to the wildlife reserve if you have problems finding the path.

4 BARBADOS WILDLIFE RESERVE

Established in 1985 primarily as a sanctuary for the Barbados green, or vervet, monkey, this 1·2 hectare reserve is also home to armadillos, agoutis, porcupines, caymans, deer, opossums, racoons and, of particular interest, a large collection of rare red-foot tortoises. It is a relaxed and relaxing place with shaded paths, a walk-in aviary and a stream

Morgan Lewis Mill is an intact reminder of the sugar cane boom days

inhabited by otters, swans and ducks.

Cut across the road to Farley Hill.

5 FARLEY HILL NATIONAL PARK

An avenue of royal palms and casuarina trees leads to the ruins of a mansion built in 1861 for the visit of Prince Albert, Duke of Edinburgh. It was once one of the grandest buildings on the island.

Pause to enjoy the view from the grounds then take the path to the right of the house which eventually leads through a steep gully back to the road to Bleak House.

Morgan Lewis Mill. Open: daily, 9am–5pm. Admission charge.
St Nicholas Abbey. Open: Monday to Friday, 10am–3pm. Admission charge.
Barbados Wildlife Reserve. Open: daily, 10am–5pm. Admission charge. For further details contact Barbados National Trust (tel: 436 9033).

St Vincent and the Grenadines

ST VINCENT

The first name was the best: Youroumei, 'the beauty of the rainbow in the valleys' was what the original inhabitants called this mountainous island of volcanic peaks and lush green valleys. First came the Ciboney people, followed by the Arawaks and then the Caribs, who took in many of the colonial settlers' escaped slaves; in the north of St Vincent today it is still possible to meet the descendants of this alliance.

Despite the number of visitors who pass through its airports, St Vincent itself has missed out on the Caribbean tourist boom. Most visitors seem to prefer the white-sand beaches, the coral reefs and the perfect sailing conditions round the Grenadines to its south. However, St Vincent rewards anyone curious enough to look, with some of the greenest, most fertile, most spectacular landscapes in the Caribbean.

KINGSTOWN

The busy commercial hub of Kingstown (population 25,000) can hardly be described as a picturesque town. However, it has a lively market, a bustling port and a few interesting old colonial buildings.

Kingstown view, with the towers of the Roman Catholic church

Kingstown's Churches

St George's Anglican Cathedral is the principal church of the diocese of the Windward Isles. The oldest church on the island, its memorial stones tell something of St Vincent's early colonial history, particularly the slab set into the centre aisle which commemorates a British soldier killed in the war against the Caribs. The stained-glass window with the red angel is said to have been commissioned by Queen Victoria for St Paul's Cathedral in London, but she rejected it saying that in the Bible, angels wear white.

The sombre-looking façade of the **Methodist Church** is a little off-putting. Inside, however, it is surprisingly colourful, with painted pillars, bright stained-glass windows and a crystal chandelier. **St Mary's Roman Catholic Church** is a remarkable kaleidoscope of styles – Gothic, Romanesque, baroque, Renaissance – with arches, turrets and towers. It was created by Dom Charles Verbeke, a Benedictine priest from Belgium who used pictures of the famous cathedrals of Europe as his models.
St George's Cathedral, Granby Street; Methodist Church, Grenville Street; St Mary's, Grenville Street. Open access.

ARROWROOT
Under British rule sugar was king; as that industry began to die out, arrowroot became the island's leading crop. St Vincent is still one of the world's leading producers of this odd crop, which was once used as a starch and food-thickening agent but which has found a new role coating computer paper.

ST VINCENT AND THE GRENADINES

BOTANIC GARDENS AND MUSEUM

Established in 1765, the oldest botanical gardens in the western hemisphere grew out of an advertisement in a British newspaper offering a reward to anyone who could 'cultivate a spot in the West Indies in which plants, useful in medicine and profitable as articles of commerce, might be propagated, and where nurseries of the valuable productions of Asia and other distant parts might be formed for the benefit of His Majesty's colonies'.

General Melville, governor of the island at the time, answered the challenge by clearing the land at his own expense, and eventually his gardens were designated an official out-station of Kew Gardens in London. The 50-guinea reward the initial advertisement had offered was finally claimed in 1774 by Dr George Young, the gardens' first superintendent.

Give thanks and praise is the excellent name of this fishing boat

Enter the gardens through the ornate gates and cross a bridge near a huge rubber tree and some magnificent baobabs. The prize exhibit is a breadfruit tree, near the north entrance, which dates from 1793. This is from one of the original plants brought to the Caribbean from Tahiti by Captain Bligh (of *The Bounty*).

On the west side of the garden the National Museum houses a collection of pre-Columbian artefacts found on the island and a section of a canoe used to retrace the route of the Amerindians from South America. Close to the nursery, the Nicholls Wildlife Complex has an aviary which houses the rare St Vincent parrot. Beyond the path at the northern end of the gardens is the old Governor-General's house built by General Melville in 1835.

In the north of Kingstown (tel: 457 1003). Open: Monday to Friday, 7am–4pm; Saturday, 7am–11am; Sunday 7am–6pm. Admission free. (Museum open: Wednesday, 8am–11am and Saturday 4pm–6pm, or by arrangement.)

FALLS OF BALEINE

A stunning example of nature's beneficence to St Vincent, the Falls of Baleine are usually reached by a two-hour trip along the west coast from Kingstown (with a stop to snorkel or swim at Anchor reef). The boat anchors off a black-sand beach 500m or so from the falls.

The falls tumble in an avalanche of spray, about 20m from a steep gorge on the north side of Soufrière volcano, into a huge, rock-lined pool. A refreshing swim can usually be taken here.
In the very north of the island. The tourist office in Kingstown has details of tour operators. Canvas shoes or some kind of protection for feet is advisable.

Some of Kingstown's old houses remain. This one is in Lower Bay Street

FORT CHARLOTTE

Set on a 200m hill, once known as Berkshire Hill, Fort Charlotte commands a fabulous view across Kingstown Bay towards the Grenadines. It was named after the wife of King George II and was built between 1791 and 1812. As proof of the problems the island's Caribs used to cause the British forces, Fort Charlotte's guns point inwards rather than out to sea. There is a small museum inside detailing the struggle against the Caribs.
3km west of Kingstown. Museum open: weekdays, 9am–5pm. Admission charge.

MESOPOTAMIA VALLEY

One of the most fertile areas in the Caribbean, the upper slopes of Mesopotamia are thick with tree ferns, bamboo, nutmeg, cocoa and coconut, while the lower reaches are the island's larder of bananas, plantains, breadfruit, eddoes and dasheen.

This valley was once an important Carib settlement; they knew it as Marriaqua, meaning 'married waters' – all the rivers which drain into the valley come together before flowing into the sea over the rocks of the Yambou Gorge.
In the central southeast of the island.

WHALE-WATCHING

Whale- and dolphin-watching is becoming increasingly popular in many parts of the world, including the Caribbean. In particular, many people come to the islands to see the humpback whales that winter here to calve and mate. The Grenadines and St Vincent are among the best locations for watching these magnificent creatures, but sightings of humpback whales, sperm whales, spotted dolphins and bottle-nosed dolphins can be had from cruise ships and ferries in many areas. For the more dedicated whale enthusiast there are also locally based cruises, the details of which can be obtained from the Eastern Caribbean Tourist Association at 220 E 42nd Street, New York, NY 10017, USA. Whale study trips are operated in the Grenadines by Great Expeditions, Box 46499, Station G, Vancouver, BC V6K 1R4, Canada and Ocean Voyages Inc, 1709 Bridgeway, Sausalito, CA94965, USA.

Safe haven in Admiralty Harbour, Bequia

THE GRENADINES

The three dozen little islands and cays which make up St Vincent's Grenadines are for many people a vision of the perfect Caribbean getaway. Eight of them are inhabited and each one is different in character and in atmosphere. In geographical order, south from St Vincent:

BEQUIA

Just 14km due south of St Vincent, Bequia is the largest of the Grenadines with about 5,000 inhabitants within its 18 sq km. Its name comes from an old Carib word meaning 'Island of the Clouds' – but usually the clouds skid straight past.

The island has long been associated with skilled seafarers, boat-builders and fishermen. Some of the islanders trace their ancestry back to Scots sailors, many of whom had connections with the whaling industry, and even now islanders will set off in their little boats, harpoon at the ready, whenever a whale is sighted – although they seldom catch it.

Port Elizabeth, the capital, is a charming, peaceful town gathered round the safe haven of Admiralty Bay, busy with visiting yachts. This is where most of the visitor accommodation is berthed and the usual route around town is a small broken-down concrete path which hugs the waterline, or one of the out-board-driven water taxis. Some of the island's best beaches can be found at the southern end of Admiralty Bay, such as Princess Margaret Beach and Lower Bay, where half the island seems to gather on a Sunday afternoon.

On the other side of the island is the small fishing village and whaling community of **Paget Farm** and **Friendship Bay** where the notorious Captain Kidd is said to have lain in wait for passing ships. On the southern tip of the island there is a very strange collection of stone houses built into the cliffs, known as Moonhole. There is a superb view over the Grenadines from Bequia's own mountain, 244m **Mount Pleasant**.

MUSTIQUE

An hour's sail from Bequia and 29km from St Vincent, Mustique has a jet-set reputation that stretches far beyond these shores, thanks to a Scottish landowner with a taste for the relaxed Caribbean life. The Honourable Colin Tennant (now known as Lord Glenconner) purchased the island when the tourist industry was in its infancy. Until then, Mustique (the name comes from the French for mosquito) had been owned by the descendants of the Hazell family

View from the ferry at Bequia

who had acquired it in 1835 for growing sugar cane and cotton. Glenconner had a different business in mind and in 1968 formed the Mustique Company with a view to turning it into a private tourist destination.

Under the direction of the celebrated designer and architect Oliver Messel, several luxurious villas were built, many with Messel's theatrical trademarks. There are now some 80 or so very expensive houses on Mustique, including the holiday homes of Princess Margaret, Mick Jagger, David Bowie and Raquel Welch.

Mustique is the most manicured of the islands in the group and is one of the few Grenadines with real paved roads. There are several good beaches, such as **Macaroni** in the southeast; and the snorkelling is so good the government of St Vincent has declared the sea and the coral reefs for 1,000 metres around Mustique a conservation area.

CANOUAN

Very popular with the yachting set, Canouan is a small, tranquil, largely unspoilt scrubby island of low, rounded hills surrounded by superb beaches and stunning coral reefs, 40km south of St Vincent. Named by the Caribs after its sea-turtles, it has a permanent population of just 1,000 inhabitants, mostly making their living from tourism, fishing and farming.

CARRIACOU, see pages 118–19.

MAYREAU

This 4 sq km island 54km from St Vincent has missed out on much of the development which has been visited on the other inhabited Grenadines. It is still privately owned by a Vincentian family and until the Salt Whistle Bay Hotel opened in the late 1980s there were no facilities on the island at all. It still manages without cars (or, for that matter, roads).

It is a short hike up to the main population centre on top of **Station Hill**, where there is a fine view over the Tobago Cays and Horseshoe Reef. This is also where you find the island's tiny Roman Catholic church with its miniature belfry. **Salt Whistle Bay** on the northwest is one of the smoothest anchorages in the Grenadines and is fine for swimming, as is **Saline Bay** on the southwest coast with its long beach. Divers are attracted to the wreck of a British gunboat on the west coast 300 metres off **Grand Col Point**.

Local sailboats provide a romantic way of exploring the Grenadines

TOBAGO CAYS

A group of deserted islands east of Mayreau, accessible only by boat, the Tobago Cays offer some of the best snorkelling in the eastern Caribbean with huge shoals of colourful tropical fish swimming through the coral reefs. Non-swimmers too come to laze on its brilliant white beaches, paddle in the clear blue shallows and walk along its deserted shores.

The Tobago Cays were recently declared a national park by the government in St Vincent, permanent moorings have been laid to protect the reefs from careless anchors, and divers are being asked not to take any of the fragile coral. The best time to visit is at low tide when the current is at its weakest and, if travelling independently, either early in the morning or late in the afternoon after the day-trippers have moved on.

UNION ISLAND

It used to be known as the 'Gateway to the Grenadines' and Union Island (64km from St Vincent) is still more of a hub for connecting airline passengers with their yachts and ferries and for provisioning boats than a destination in its own right. Perhaps this has something to do with its reputation as the least friendly of the Grenadines. It was first mentioned in

The Grenadines offer some of the most luxurious cruising in the Caribbean

despatches in 1654 when two Frenchmen were marooned here against their will. A year later it had become one of the area's leading cotton producers.

Union Island's dramatic jagged profile includes the highest peak of the Grenadines, **Mount Tabor** (305m), and hiking is a popular pastime for visitors. There are two principal communities, **Clifton** in the southeast, and **Ashton** in the south. The best beaches, at **Chatham Bay**, **Richmond Bay** and **Bloody Bay**, are in the north and west and the best snorkelling is around **Frigate Island** in the south.

PALM ISLAND AND PETIT ST VINCENT

Either of these privately owned resort islands could be described as the epitome of Carribean escapism. **Palm**, 400m east of Union, used to be known as Prune Island, but that name did not suit the purposes of John Caldwell who spotted it when he was sailing in the Grenadines 30 years ago. In those days there were just swamps and mosquitoes on the 44 hectare island but, after negotiating a 99-year lease at US$1 a year (with a renewal option of another 99 years afterwards), he and his wife Mary drained the worst of the swamps, planted more than 2,000 palm trees and countless other tropical plants, and built a hotel (not that you would know it was there from a distance, so carefully are the cottages hidden amongst the trees).

Half of **Petit St Vincent** (or PSV as it is more commonly known) has been developed, the other half has been left in its natural state. Like Palm Island, PSV is a private resort island where guests are guaranteed seclusion. If they require room service, they run a yellow flag up the pole beside their cottage. If they wish to be left alone they hoist the red.

UNDER WATER

Pretty though the Caribbean islands are, the scenery above the waterline is often matched by the brilliant colours of the coral reefs and their tropical inhabitants below the sea. This is one of the most exciting destinations in the world for divers and the islands are equipped to meet their every need. Prime dive sites are well marked around the islands; important areas are protected with a conservation status and, here and there, new reefs are created for divers to explore by the careful positioning of wrecked cars and the sinking of unserviceable ships.

Learning to dive on holiday is a simple business and island schools usually belong to the Professional Association of Diving Instructors (PADI) or the National Association of Underwater Instructors (NAUI), but it is worth checking credentials in advance. The first lesson usually takes place on dry land and covers the theory of a successful dive; then

Coral reefs are very easily damaged by boats and by clumsy divers. Left: sponges on coral Right: swimming with a stingray Below: cherub fish

the novice and instructor take to the hotel swimming pool with a chance to try on the equipment in a safe environment. Supervised dives follow at sea and by the end of the holiday most learners are presented with a certificate of competence.

More experienced divers, who already have their certificates, find all the facilities they need to explore the reefs as soon as they arrive. If the hotel itself does not have a dive shop, the tourist office has a list of the nearest agencies. Note that spear fishing is banned in many places.

If diving does not appeal, snorkelling is an exciting alternative. Most hotels have equipment for their guests or for hire to non-residents; plastic charts are sold in many shops and hotel boutiques to help identify the brilliant underwater world. Sometimes the sight is so hypnotic, the swimmer loses track of time so it is important to wear a T-shirt to prevent a nasty sunburn. Many dive operations hire out underwater cameras. Do remember that coral is fragile and a few clumsily placed feet can bring to an end thousands of years of growth on that part of the reef, with all the disruption that that would cause to the marine life which depends on it. Those who prefer to look at the underwater world without getting wet may go for a trip on a glass-bottomed boat or in one of the more sophisticated Atlantis tourist submarines on Barbados and St Thomas (see page 161).

Grenada

Grenada not only looks good, it smells good too. A hint of nutmeg here, cinammon or saffron there – not for nothing is Grenada known as the Spice Island of the Caribbean. It is immensely attractive, with a lush jagged mountainous terrain tumbling down to hidden coves and, here and there, long swathes of white-sand beaches that reveal a gentler more accessible face.

ST GEORGE'S

Grenada's capital is supremely pretty, with whitewashed, red- and green-roofed houses rising step by step behind the perfect deep-water anchorage. Most of the commercial buildings are on the first level, on the broad Carenage that sweeps round the bay. This is the place to sit on one of the old cannons and watch small cargo ships loading up with fruit and vegetables.

The island's most interesting old colonial buildings are to be found in the streets which climb above the Carenage: **Government House** (1802), a fine example of Georgian colonial architecture, **York House** (1801) home to Grenada's supreme court, the **Registry Building** (1780); and **St George's churches** – St Andrew's

MARKET DOLLS

In nearly every market in the eastern Caribbean, traders with time to spare make market dolls from scraps of material and odds and ends. They are highly collectable, bright, colourful souvenirs of a holiday in the sun.

Cruise ship dwarfing St George's

Presbytery, known as the Scots' Kirk (1884), St George's Roman Catholic Church (1884), St George's Methodist Church (1820) and St George's Anglican Church which, although it was rebuilt in 1825, is lined with plaques showing St George in the 18th and 19th centuries. *Access to Government House, York House and the Registry Building is limited. The churches are open to the public at all times.*

Fort Frederick

There used to be four forts on the ridge of Richmond Hill overlooking St George's. Fort Frederick, between the ruins of Fort Matthew and Fort Adolphus, was begun in 1779 soon after the French wrenched the island from Britain; it was completed in 1791 after the British won it back. There are spectacular views to be had from the fort's old parade ground and battlements. *Richmond Hill, St George's. Open access.*

> **REVOLUTION**
>
> Grenada gained independence from Britain in 1974 but five years later a bloodless coup led by the militant Maurice Bishop overthrew Governor Sir Eric Gairy. The United States became concerned when the People's Revolutionary Party led by Bishop began to accept assistance from Cuba and eventually, fearing a new stronghold of communism in Uncle Sam's backyard, they invaded in 1983 with the aim of bringing political stability to the island. This move was welcomed by many people on Grenada, for by then the People's Revolution had gone horribly wrong. The island has been politically stable ever since.

GRENADA

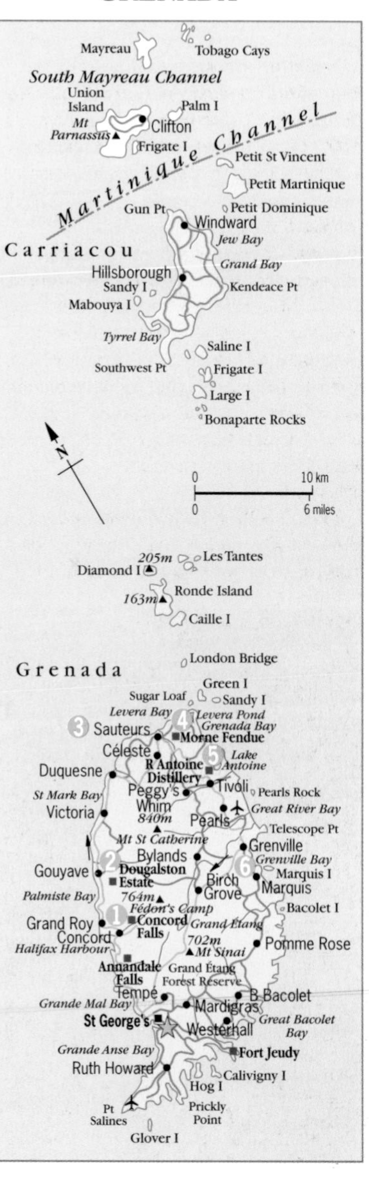

Fort George

The entrance to St George's Harbour is guarded by one of the best preserved of the six forts which used to protect the city. Built originally as Fort Royal by the French in 1706, it was later seized by the British and renamed after the reigning monarch. Set on a promontory, with walls more than a metre thick, it offers a superb view over the rooftops of St George's. At one time it is thought all of the city's forts were connected by a series of tunnels and there are still underground passageways to be seen below Fort George. In more recent times the fort played a part in the final chapters of the 1983 revolution when Maurice Bishop and several of his supporters were murdered in its courtyard.

Church Street, St George's. The outer courtyard is open daily, 6am–7pm.

Market Square

A steep walk up from the Carenage, or a short drive through the 1895 Sendall tunnel, St George's Market Square looks like a film set, particularly on a Saturday morning when the pastel buildings, the brightly dressed traders with their colourful sunshades and brilliant island produce makes it one of the most photogenic scenes in the islands.

National Museum

Set into the foundations of an old French army barracks and prison built in 1704, this small island museum features artefacts from archaeological excavations around Grenada, including many that date back to the time of the Ciboneys, the Arawaks and Caribs. There is a natural history section describing some of the wildlife on the island, costumes from the Grenada carnival, and old steam-driven engines from the sugar

Schoolchildren Grenada style

plantation days.
Corner of Young Street, St George's (tel: 440 3725). Open: Monday to Friday, 9am–3pm; Saturday, 10.30am–2pm. Admission charge.

AROUND GRENADA

ANNANDALE FALLS

An accessible place for a cooling dip, the Annandale Falls are reached by a short detour from the main Grand Etang road, just 15 minutes from St George's. A mountain stream cascades 15m into a natural pool surrounded by elephant ears, liannas and other tropical flora. There are changing rooms near by and a centre where islanders sell spices and local craftwork.

GRAND ANSE BEACH

It is hard to imagine this, one of the best-known strips of sand in the Caribbean, as the scene of the American invasion in 1983. The fine white coral sands are the most popular on the island, and there are several hotels along the edge. At the southernmost point of the bay is Quarantine Point, so called because of the hospital constructed on the promontory in the 19th century for soldiers stricken by smallpox. The government converted them into an inexpensive holiday resort for islanders but the complex was not a success and fell into disrepair.
South of St George's.

GRAND ETANG FOREST RESERVE

Part of the jagged range of mountains forming Grenada's volcanic spine, the Grand Etang is a water-filled crater some 580m above sea-level. Many islanders claim the lake is bottomless. One of

Grand Anse beach

Grenada's highest peaks, Mount Qua Qua, rises to the north while the forests around the lake abound with a rich diversity of wildlife.

A short distance across the road from the lake, the Forestry Department has established a visitors' interpretation centre with displays and information on the self-guided nature trails in the area. One of the best is a three-hour hike known as the Seven Sisters Trail which leads through cultivated land, then virgin forest to a series of waterfalls dropping down into a large pool, perfect for a refreshing swim after an arduous walk.
Take the inland road east of St George's. For further information contact the Grenada Forestry Department (tel:440 2248).

Annandale Falls, one of Grenada's beautiful inland swimming spots

LA SAGESSE NATURE CENTRE AND MARQUIS

The first Europeans to settle on Grenada chose an area known as La Sagesse in the southeast corner of the island. Now part of the national parks system, this once-private estate includes three fine beaches, coral reefs, a mangrove estuary teeming with birdlife, a salt pond and interesting examples of shore-front forest and thorn scrub cactus woodland. As its name suggests, the area was settled by the French; the village of Marquis further north was once the island's capital and was the scene of an infamous massacre of British inhabitants during the Fédon insurrection of 1795.

An enjoyable half hour scenic hike from the village, along the banks of the river, leads to the Marquis River Waterfall.

La Sagesse Nature Centre guesthouse (tel: 444 6458). Co-ordinates nature treks in the area.

WESTERHALL

The residential area near by is popular with expatriates and retired Grenadians. Indeed, the whole of the south coast from Point Salines, where the international airport is located, to Great Bacolet Bay is made up of a network of hilly peninsulas and secluded coves that hide some of the most sought-after real estate on the island.

Take the main road south of St George's.

For attractions north of St George's and at the top of the island, see page 120.

CARRIACOU

The largest island in the Grenadine chain, Carriacou – along with her sister Petit Martinique – belongs to Grenada 37km to the south. In its earliest colonial days, Carriacou was an important sugar and cotton producer, although that is hard to imagine now that extensive erosion has contributed to its rather dry terrain. Later the island also became known for the quality of its boat-building, thanks largely to a group of shipwrights who arrived from Glasgow in Scotland to build cargo ships for transporting the island's produce overseas.

Surprisingly there are 130km of road on Carriacou, originally built by the French so that they could move their artillery quickly around the island to head off British attacks.

HILLSBOROUGH

The principal town on the island, Hillsborough is built on the curve of a wide bay with its Main Street running parallel to the shore. A small **museum** located in the oldest house features a collection of Amerindian artefacts.

Carriacou Museum. Open: Monday to Friday, 9.30am–2.30pm. Admission free.

BIG DRUM

A particularly interesting social phenomenon on Carriacou is the Big Drum dance, performed on special occasions. Many of the islanders claim they can trace their ancestry directly to the African tribe to which they belong; the Big Drum is a way of communicating with their ancestors.

PETIT MARTINIQUE

Approximately 600 people live on the 227m high volcanic cone of Petit Martinique, 45km from Grenada. During the development of the resort on Petit St-Vincent, just 1,000 metres away, they proved a useful pool of labour. The main settlement used to be divided by a gully running down the hill; one side, where the ship-owners lived, was known as White Town, the other as Black Town. These days the distinctions between the two sides are blurred. Most of the income on the island is derived from fishing and boat-building.

Grenada's other islands include **Kick'em Jenny** (Diamond Island), **Caille I** with its ruined whaling station, **The Sisters**, **Ile de Ronde** (the only other inhabited island), **Les Tantes** and **London Bridge** – really only an islet.

Street scene in Carriacou

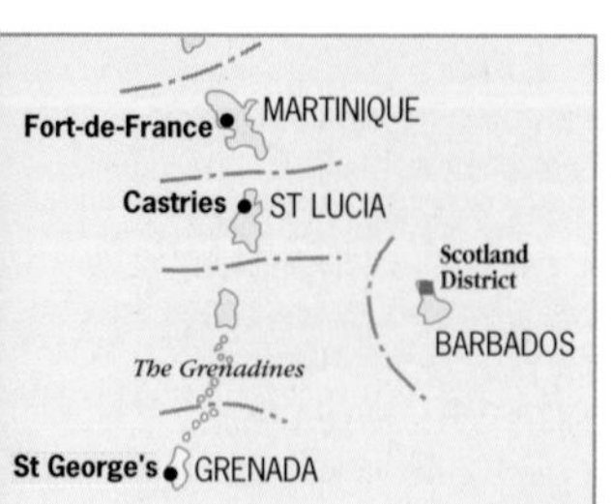

Grenada Drive

A drive up the west coast from St George's, round the top of the island and returning by the spectacular route through the Grand Etang. For the drive route, see the main Grenada map on page 115. ***Allow most of the day.***

Leave St George's by the northern Esplanade, cross the small bridge on the outskirts of town and continue along the west coast road to Halifax Harbour, then follow the signs along the rutted single lane track to the Concord Falls.

1 CONCORD FALLS

When the Black Bay River reaches the Concord Valley between Mount Qua Qua and the coast it forms a series of three picturesque waterfalls. The first can be crowded at weekends so persevere to the second, on the bend of the river or, even better, take a swim at the highest fall, known as Fontainebleu.

Return to the main road and continue towards Gouyave.

2 DOUGALSTON ESTATE

Immediately before Gouyave, follow signs to Dougalston Estate, one of the island's oldest nutmeg plantations, where visitors can see nutmeg, mace, cinammon, cloves and allspice. The country's principal nutmeg-processing station can also be visited in Gouyave itself. Beyond Gouyave the road begins to get exciting and, at times, where it hugs the sea under cliffs, you may well feel the spray through the open car window.

Continue to the fishing community of Victoria at the foot of the island's highest peak, Mount St Catherine; then, when the road turns inland at Duquesne, follow the signs for Sauteurs.

3 SAUTEURS

After climbing the hill through the main section of town turn left and stop by the

Betty Mascoll's Morne Fendue

Mace drying. This spice is the dried outer husk of nutmeg

police station and the Roman Catholic church. This is the infamous Caribs' Leap where, in 1651, the last of the Caribs plunged 300m to their death rather than surrender to the French.

Sauteurs Bay, to the west of town, is a good area for a picnic or a swim but a better option for lunch is to follow the signs to Morne Fendue, southeast of town.

4 MORNE FENDUE

This old plantation house was built in 1908 using hand-cut stones and a mortar of lime and molasses. Betty Mascoll, the owner of the property, is famous for her lunches featuring traditional island specialities. From the veranda of the house, there is a good view to Levera National Park. If visiting Morne Fendue for lunch it is important to reserve a place in advance (tel. 440 9330)

Return to the main road and after a while follow the signs to the distillery.

5 RIVER ANTOINE DISTILLERY

Rum can be seen being made here, in much the same way as in the 18th century, with the river still used to turn the old waterwheel. From here a detour may be taken on foot to Lake Antoine, a peaceful place surrounded by gentle countryside in a long-dead volcanic crater.

Return to the main road and drive south to Grenville.

6 GRENVILLE

The second largest town on the island, Grenville has its own busy market. It is less frenetic than St George's (but also less photogenic). A boat-building and fishing centre, Grenville also has a spice-processing factory which can be visited by the public.

Take the spectacular mountainous inland route - twisty and narrow but well-surfaced - across Grand Etang and back to St George's.

Trinidad

It might seem bizarre to describe an island of the size and the reputation of Trinidad as an undiscovered gem, but the truth is that this 4,900 sq km island with 1·2 million inhabitants, the most southern of the Caribbean chain, has barely begun to achieve its true tourist potential. There is more here for the visitor than on half a dozen of the smaller islands put together; fabulous mountain scenery, exotic wildlife (much of it to be seen nowhere else in the Caribbean), a rich multi-ethnic culture and, once a year, a world-famous-carnival, the liveliest party in the Caribbean.

There are just 11km between Trinidad and its neighbour Venezuela at the narrowest point in the sea, and Trinidad acted as a stepping stone for many tribes of Arawaks and Caribs on their migrations from South America to the other islands. They called it, appropriately enough, given its exotic wildlife, Iere, 'Land of the Hummingbird'.

PORT OF SPAIN

This busy city might come as a bit of a shock after some of the smaller island capitals. Tourism seems of little consequence here; this is a living, breathing port with business on its mind. It is extremely busy and very crowded. Nevertheless, from a vantage point somewhere on the Northern Range it still manages to look good, with the lush open parkland of the Savannah in the foreground and the broad channel of the Gulf of Paria behind.

Beer hoarding

Cathedral of the Immaculate Conception

The Roman Catholic cathedral, built in the shape of the cross, is fashioned from blue stone from the Laventile Hills. When it was completed in 1832 it stood beside the sea but land reclamation has left it well inland. A thorough renovation in 1984 saw the addition of the 14 Stations of the Cross in Italian marble and 16 stained-glass windows from Ireland.

At the intersection of Independence Square and George Street. Open access.

Frederick Street

The most important shopping street on the island is also one of the best places in the Caribbean for people-watching. The whole kaleidoscope of races which make up modern Trinidad can be seen here. The liveliest section is selling bright Indian cloth from Madras at the lower end of the street, close to Independence Square, where the storekeepers try to lure customers away from the opposition by blasting Trinidad's favourite calypsos out across the street.

Situated between Queen's Park Savannah and Independence Square.

Independence Square
Whatever else it might be, this is certainly not a square. A busy thoroughfare, it is more like two broad avenues stretching between the port and the city's eastern fringe. It was laid out in 1816 but the more modern office blocks on its southern side bear testament to the importance of Trinidad's oil business. Half way along its length, there is a statue of Arthur Andrew Cipriani, a former mayor of the city and pioneer of the independence movement.
In the south of the city.

Drinking coconut water

TRINIDAD

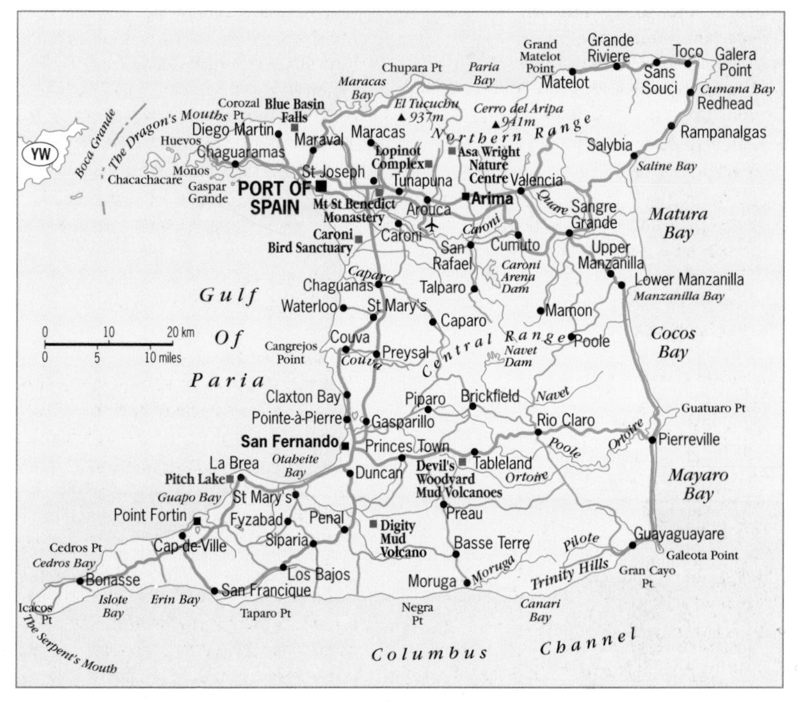

THE PEOPLE OF TRINIDAD

Trinidad was ceded to Britain in 1802 and when slavery was abolished 32 years later a large workforce was recruited from colonial India to work the land. East Indians, as they are called, now account for half the population on the island.

Queen's Park Savannah

A vast grassy area of 80 hectares, the Queen's Park Savannah is one of the most generous tracts of open land within the boundaries of any city in the world. Governor Woodford laid it out in 1820 as a common for the purposes of general recreation, and that is how it is still used today. Here Trinidadians exercise their horses at dawn, go jogging, stroll arm in arm, practice tai chi and karate, play football and cricket (there are 26 pitches) or just 'lime out' in the shade of the many trees – bordering the park are royal palms, cannonball trees, yellow pouis, flamboyants and African tulips. With a circumference of 5km, there is enough room for everyone.

This is also one of the best places to try local food from the vendors around the park's perimeter. Every February the Savannah stages the main events of the Trinidad Carnival. (See also page 128.)

The Red House

This neo-Rennaissance building is home to the Trinidad parliament and several government departments. It was originally built in 1844 and painted red in 1897 to celebrate Queen Victoria's Diamond Jubilee. Burned down in 1903 as part of a protest against the colonial government, it was quickly rebuilt, but was damaged once again in the summer of 1990 when Muslim militants took the prime minister and many of the island's members of parliament hostage.

On the west side of Woodford Square. Limited access.

Parliament building, called the Red House

Woodford Square

After a fire in 1808 destroyed much of the old Port of Spain, the young British governor of the island, Ralph Woodford, set about rebuilding it with considerable enthusiasm and style. Over the years Woodford Square, named after him, has been the focal point for one of Trinidad's favourite preoccupations: talking politics. Even now anyone with a political bone to pick stands up and chews it in the area under the old trees known jokingly as the University of Woodford Square. On the south side of Woodford Square is the **Cathedral of the Holy Trinity**, the Anglican cathedral built by Woodford and finished in 1818. The carved roof supported by mahogany beams is a replica of Westminster Hall in London. To the north is City Hall, built in 1961 to replace an earlier building also destroyed by fire.

Situated between Frederick Street and Abercromby Street.

A view of Queen's Park Savannah

ASA WRIGHT NATURE CENTRE

Deep in the rainforest on the slopes of the Northern Range, the Asa Wright Centre is a magnet for nature lovers. It was established in 1967 on the Spring Hill Estate, a former coffee, fruit and cocoa plantation, as a centre for recreation and study as well as for the protection and conservation of tropical wildlife. The balcony of the old estate house, now a hotel, overlooks the dark green tangle of the Arima Valley and offers excellent opportunities to view the

BIRDING ON TRINIDAD AND TOBAGO

Trinidad and Tobago have gained world-class reputations as superb sites for birdwatching (or 'birding').One of the reasons for the wealth of species found on these tiny islands is their proximity to South America. Consequently, almost all the bird families found on the mainland also occur here in a comparatively small area with a relatively stress-free environment. The islands are also a staging post for migrant birds heading south from North America to escape the winter. Many of the migrants stay for the duration of the northern winter, arriving in September and staying until April.

Although solo birdwatching can be extremely rewarding, many first-time visitors choose to employ the services of a 'birding' guide to help them get started and to locate the best sites and species. Not every guide with a pair of binoculars is going to be an expert, but the best are listed – together with phone numbers – in a small but popular book entitled *The Birders Guide to Trinidad and Tobago* by W L Murphy. One local guide with a particularly good reputation is Winston Nanaan, who can not only take you to see many of the terrestrial specialities but also operates boats to see the scarlet ibises.

Blue sea and white surf at Maracas beach

birdlife of the centre at close quarters. Of particular interest is the only easily accessible breeding colony of oil birds in the Caribbean.

There are five trails varying in difficulty, starting from the house: the Mot Mot Trail, in search of a bird with a very strange repertoire of calls; the Cahaconia Trail, which is noted for its display of butterflies; the Bamboo Valley Trail; the Heliconia Trail; and the more exacting Adventure Trail.

13km north of the town of Arima (tel:667 4655). Open: daily, 9am–5pm. Admission charge.

CARONI BIRD SANCTUARY

In one of the most glorious wildlife displays in the Caribbean, hundreds of magnificent scarlet ibises fly over from Venezuela every evening at sunset to roost on one small area, a tangled mass of mangrove within the Caroni Bird Sanctuary. The sanctuary covers 55 hectares of lagoon and swamp and is a place of great stillness and beauty. Stable flat-bottomed boats make their way along the Blue River in the late afternoon while guides describe the species of mangrove and identify the birds feeding on the banks along the way.

The sanctuary has 150 species of birds, 80 kinds of fish and a variety of reptiles. As the sun begins to set the boats tie up a safe distance from the roost but close enough to allow superb photo-opportunities.

10km south from Port of Spain, access is west of the Uriah Butler Highway. Visits are usually late in the afternoon, from around 4pm until 7pm, depending on the time of year; the birds are most numerous outside the nesting season, between September and March. Details of tour organisers from the island's tourist offices.

CHAGUARAMAS

The Chaguaramas Peninsula and its islands are part of the Chaguaramas National Park, whose highest peak is the

539m Mount Catherine. There is still much evidence of its occupation by American forces during World War II. A popular day trip from the capital, the island of Gaspar Grande, 1.5km offshore, boasts a network of caves with stalactites and stalagmites which can be viewed alongside floodlit walkways.
Due west of Port of Spain.

MARACAS BAY
Trinidad's most popular beach is a 35-minute scenic drive from Port of Spain along the north coast road, popularly referred to as the Skyline Highway. It is busy at weekends, particularly Sundays, and on full-moon nights. There is a good viewpoint just before the road dips down towards Maracas; often there is a local musician waiting here to serenade those who stop with personal calypsos improvised on the spot. Several stalls near the car park at Maracas Bay sell the Trinidadian speciality, shark-and-bake, fried over a coalpot. If the beach at Maracas is too busy, Tyrico a short distance further along tends to be quieter.
On the north coast road from Port of Spain.

PITCH LAKE
Sir Walter Raleigh is credited with discovering this, the largest deposit of asphalt in the world. He used it to caulk his ships. It is a strange place. Crude oil seeping through a fault line in the sandstone 75m below ground level provides an endless supply of bitumen for roads and asphalt roofs. It is possible to walk on the surface of the 'lake', but a car would sink up to its axles in a few minutes and other objects simply disappear, only to resurface years later as the pitch slowly swirls about.
Near the coast at La Brea, south from Port of Spain. Guides are available (at a price).

Living jewel taking a breather: copper-rumped hummingbird

HUMMINGBIRDS
Few visitors to the Caribbean can fail to be captivated by the region's hummingbirds. As a group, they hold all sorts of bird world records – including having the fastest wing beats and, more surprisingly perhaps, laying the largest eggs in relation to body size. Equally remarkable are their names; visitors to the region can expect to see such exotic species as pufflegs, mangos, streamertails and woodstars. Many hotel grounds and private gardens put up feeders to attract these colourful visitors. The feeders supply sugar-water, an energy-rich food source that hummingbirds find irresistible. In the wild, they feed largely on nectar, and are important pollinating agents in South and Central America. Red is their favourite flower colour and they have even been known to investigate humans wearing red clothes in the vain hope of a meal.

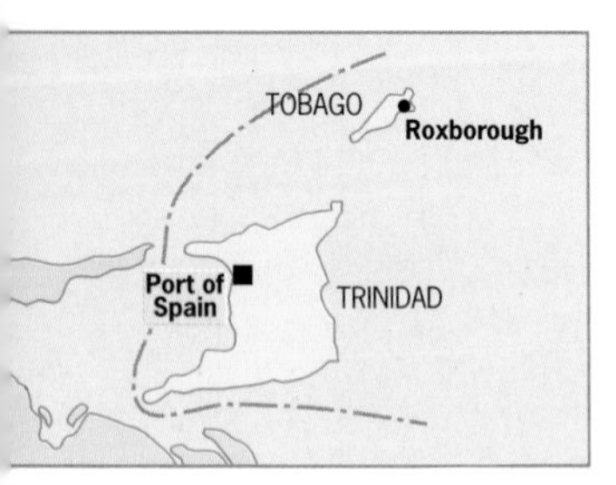

Trinidad Walk

This stroll round the Queen's Park Savannah in Port of Spain takes in many sights. Refreshments, including coconut milk, are available from vendors along the way. *Allow at least half a day.*

Start at the museum on the corner of Frederick and Keate Streets.

1 NATIONAL MUSEUM AND ART GALLERY

Founded in 1872 and housed in the Royal Victoria Institute, the gallery has a comprehensive collection of island artwork, from primitive to abstract to folklore. It includes the work of Trinidad's best-known artist, Jean Michel Cazabon. (Tel: 6236419; open Tuesday to Saturday, 10am–6pm; admission free.)

Walk along the side of Memorial Park in a clockwise direction.

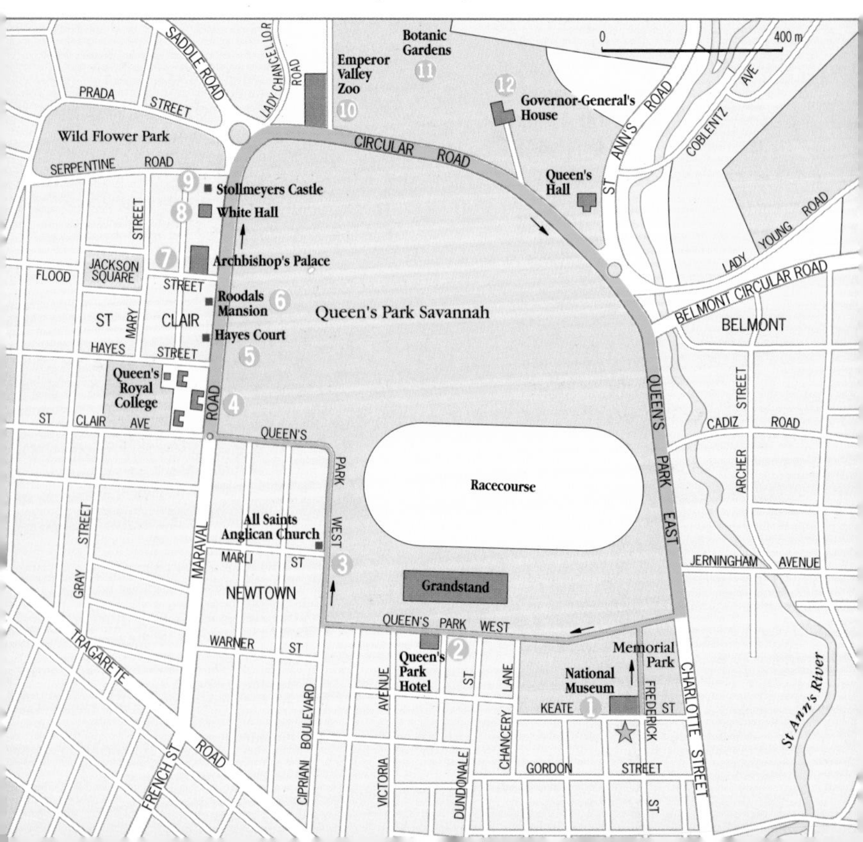

2 QUEEN'S PARK HOTEL

This was the first hotel to be built in Port of Spain and at one time was considered the best in the eastern Caribbean. Further on, note the intricate gingerbread work on no. 12 and the marble and stained-glass creation, Boissière House, at no. 26.

3 ALL SAINTS ANGLICAN CHURCH

Just after the road turns north, on the corner of Marli Street, this church is the oldest building around the Savannah, completed in 1846. Near by is the more modern American Embassy. The roundabout where Queen's Park West meets Maraval Road signals the beginning of the historic row of houses known as the Magnificent Seven.

4 QUEEN'S ROYAL COLLEGE

This is a boys' school designed by Daniel Hahn, who was also responsible for the Red House. Note the impressive clock tower.

5 HAYES COURT

The residence of the Anglican Bishop of Trinidad, this was built in 1910 by George Brown, son of a famous Chief Justice.

6 ROODALS MANSION (ALSO KNOWN AS ROOMOR)

Built in French baroque style, it has intricate slated towers and turrets and delicate wrought-iron balconies.

7 ARCHBISHOP'S PALACE

Cloisters lend a suitably ecclesiastical tone to this the official residence of the Roman Catholic Archbishop.

8 WHITE HALL

Built in a Moorish style in 1904, this was once the office of the prime minister.

Stollmeyers Castle

9 KILLARNEY (BETTER KNOWN AS STOLLMEYERS) CASTLE

Perhaps the most eccentric of the Magnificent Seven, this is a copy of a German Rhine castle.

At the top of Maraval Road, after the Wild Flower Park, turn right and continue around the Savannah.

10 EMPEROR VALLEY ZOO

The zoo was created in 1952 and named after the black and turquoise butterflies common to Trinidad. Much of the island's wildlife can be viewed here.

11 BOTANIC GARDENS

This 25 hectare garden includes mature and exotic plants which stem from the great interest in tropical flora shown in the early 19th century. The Emperor Valley Zoo and Botanical Gardens (tel: 625 2264). Open: daily, 9.30am–6pm. Admission charge.

12 GOVERNOR-GENERAL'S HOUSE

Now home to the president of Trinidad, this Italian Renaissance-style building was built in 1857. The bandstand in front of the house is often used for concerts on a Sunday evening.

Tobago

Trinidad's little sister takes great exception to being known as Trinidad's little sister. Tobago is bigger than many independent islands (Antigua for example), and the people are quick to point out the many differences between their island and their next door neighbour. For example, the relaxed atmosphere in its towns, the low crime rate, the food, the culture (Christmas is as enthusiastically celebrated on Tobago as Carnival is across the channel), the local patois – and the island's infrastructure, which has developed in recent years specifically, it seems, to cater for the tourist jetting in from Europe and North America. Good though its beach-front hotels might be, however, there is more to do on this 295 sq km island than just lie on the sand.

SCARBOROUGH

Originally known as Scarboro to the Scottish planters who settled in the area, this town is on two separate levels: most of the island's administrative buildings are to be found on Lower Scarborough, along with a new cruise ship complex and the town's bustling central market. From here the road climbs rapidly to Upper Scarborough, and then off into the surrounding hills.

The town's historical buildings include the **Tobago House of Assembly** in Piggot Street (limited access), **Gun Bridge** (the railings are made from rifle barrels) and **St Andrew's Church** in Young Street. The building (now the warden's residence) beside Scarborough Hospital, on the road up towards the fort, used to be the island prison.

TOBAGO

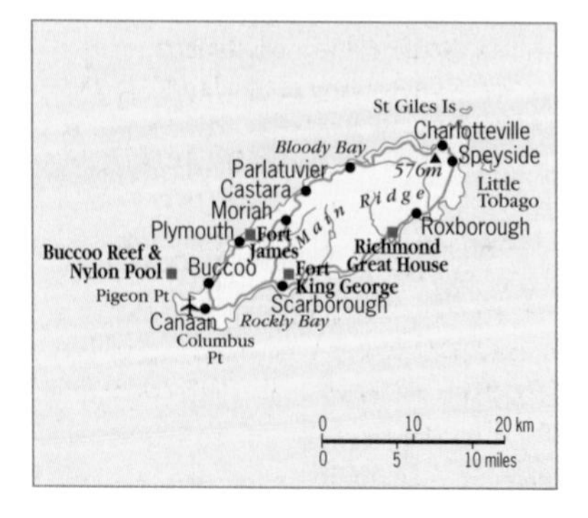

Botanic Station

A delightful garden of wide lawns, colourful flower beds, almond trees, palms, aviaries and ponds, this is a peaceful place for a late afternoon stroll. Much of the island's produce can be seen here, including 14 species of mango.

Lower Scarborough, behind the new pedestrianised precinct. Open: daily during daylight hours.

Fort King George

Commanding a secure hilltop position above the town, Fort King George was built by British forces in 1777 and is the island's main historical site. The views are superb and on a clear day it is possible to look directly across to Trinidad.

There is a small museum in the grounds, administered by the Tobago Trust, which specialises in Amerindian artefacts, including traditional burial pottery and a dug-out canoe; upstairs there is a good collection of antique charts. The old officers' mess is now a fine arts centre (with local paintings for sale), while on the grassy square in the centre of the fort complex there is a statue of two Bagonians dancing a Tobago Jig, by the island artist Louise Kimme.

The neatly landscaped grounds below Fort King George and beside the old chapel make a pleasant place to sit and enjoy the shade of an old saman tree. *Situated at the end of the road rising from Upper Scarborough. Admission free at main entrance. Museum open: Monday to Friday, 9am–5pm; Saturday and Sunday, 9am–1pm. Members of the tourist division of the island are usually on hand to offer a free tour of the fort.*

PLYMOUTH

The second town on the island, Plymouth also boasts a fort, Fort James, built by the British in 1680.

Apart from a few shops, this is a very quiet place. There is a strange tomb in the churchyard near by dedicated to one Betty Stevens who died on 25 November 1783, which has puzzled islanders for generations. The inscription reads. 'She was a mother without knowing it, and a wife without letting her husband know, except by her kind indulgences'.

In the nearby village of Golden Lane is the grave of a legendary witch, Gang Gang Sara.

Situated on the Caribbean side of the island.

PIRATES

Shortly after Columbus happened on the Caribbean islands, papal edicts declared that all land west of a line 100 leagues beyond the Azores was the property of Spain, and any foreign ships found in those waters were to be considered pirate vessels. This did not stop adventurous rogues, attracted by stories of the great wealth the Spaniards were stealing from the natives. Some of the most famous names of the day include Henry Morgan, elected 'admiral' of the buccaneers, Edward Thatch, known as Blackbeard, and Jambe de Bois, the notorious Wooden Leg of Pigeon Island, St Lucia. Many of the islands, such as Tortola and Tobago, became well-known haunts of these notorious pirates, and rumours (seldom substantiated) still abound of buried treasure.

BON ACCORD LAGOON

The shores of this lagoon are home to many different kinds of birds, including the more exotic rufous-vented chachalaca (Tobago's national bird), while the brackish water and the red mangroves sustain oysters, sponges, crabs and snails.

In the southwest, north of Pigeon Point.

BUCCOO REEF NATIONAL PARK

Tobago's best-known underwater attraction can be found in the quiet waters between Pigeon Point and Buccoo Bay. The Nylon Pool, originally known as Dan's Bank, is an area of exceptionally clear water (in places only a metre deep at low tide) where a considerable variety of corals can be seen. There is an old superstition on Tobago which suggests that its waters have healing properties and when ingested purify the skin and internal organs. A dip here is very popular among newly weds. It is advisable to wear light canvas shoes or flippers to protect the feet when swimming (however, it is also important, for the sake of the marine life, to avoid standing on the coral).

Glass-bottomed boats leave from both Pigeon Point and Store Bay. Times vary.

PARNOS VALE

Now a cocoa plantation and a rustic hillside lodge, this former sugar plantation offers a wild, natural setting for walkers and birdwatchers. The secluded cove nearby has a good coral

Boats on Buccoo Bay

reef for snorkellers and divers. To the north of the plantation, a scenic nature trail known as Warden's Road leads to Culloden Bay, while to the west, on the road between Golden Lane and Scarborough, there is an abandoned plantation with old machinery visible through the undergrowth.
On the north coast (tel: 639 2881). Open: daily, during daylight hours. Admission free.

PIGEON POINT
This is the most popular beach on the island and the island's most effective marketing tool. The vision of this narrow spit of land with a perfect palm-lined beach and a thatched dock jutting out into a calm turquoise sea has sold more holidays to Tobago than any other single image. It is private property and there is an entrance fee to be paid at the gates. There are changing facilities, T-shirt sellers and a makeshift bandstand for occasional afternoons of organised entertainment.
On the northwest coast. Open: daily, during daylight hours (later if there is a special event on). Admission charge.

SPEYSIDE AND CHARLOTTEVILLE
For a tour of two of the most picturesque Caribbean villages, see page 134–5.

TOBAGO FOREST RESERVE
The mountainous core of the island constitutes the oldest forest reserve in the western hemisphere, established by the British in 1764. The entrance to the best maintained hike, the Main Ridge Rainforest Trail, is marked beside the Bloody Bay Lookout Site. The view looks over the site of a battle so fierce the sea turned red with blood. From here, a looped trail winds down the steep hillside, through the rainforest and along a stream which empties into Bloody Bay itself, finally returning past thickets of ferns, elephant ears and gigantic bamboo under an 18m jungle-like canopy. Plenty of wildlife can be seen along the way, particularly tropical birds and brilliant butterflies.

Try to ensure that any shells you buy come from reputable sources – the creatures inside should not be killed for their shells

GOAT RACES
They have been racing goats at Buccoo village on Tobago every Easter Tuesday since 1925 and the much-valued animals even have their own racing colours. A jockey is involved, although he does not actually ride the goat. He just has to hang on to the lead for the whole of the 65m course or he risks disqualification – not to mention utter humiliation.

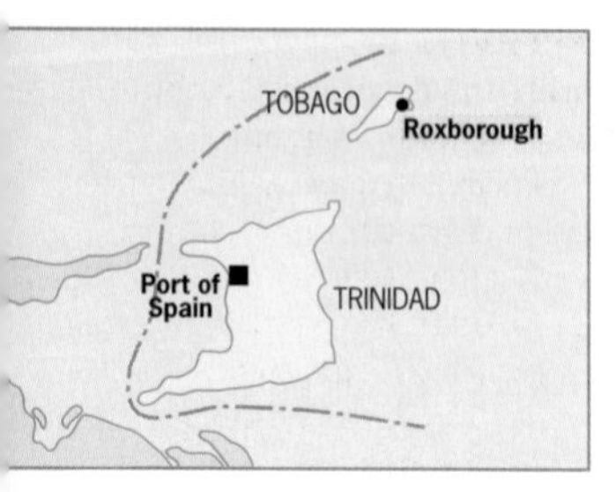

Tobago Drive

A scenic drive to the northwest of Tobago. If the road round the top has been completed then it will be possible to make a circuit back to Scarborough; otherwise some retracing of one's steps will be necessary. *Allow a full day including lunch in Speyside.*

Start from the Windward Road north of Scarborough.

1 THE WINDWARD ROAD

This route strings together a series of small fishing villages through an avenue of mango, lime and papaya trees. Note the traditional boats pulled up on the beaches. Carapuse Bay takes its name from the shell of the turtle which used to attract hunters to the area.

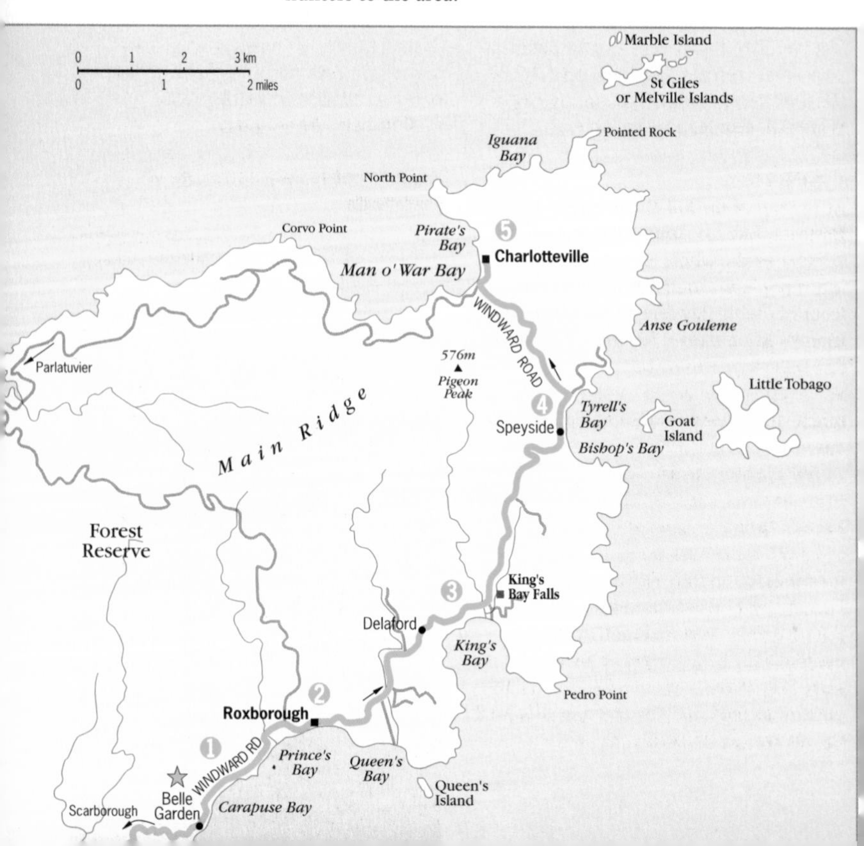

2 ROXBOROUGH

The second largest town on the island, this now peaceful community was the flashpoint for the Belmanna Riot of 1876, when former slaves, frustrated by the economic hardship imposed on them by the planters following emancipation, sprang to arms. Planters' greathouses and government buildings were burned in the rioting, until the British navy despatched a warship to restore order.

3 KING'S BAY

There are three waterfalls along this stretch of coast. The King's Bay Falls are the highest on the island with pools suitable for bathing (depending on recent rains) and with a car park and changing facilities. Follow the signs at the cocoa plantation. Alternatively, a good 50 minutes' rugged walk leads to the Argyll Waterfall. Guides are available.

4 SPEYSIDE

At the top of the hill above Speyside, the Batteaux Bay Lookout offers superb views over the whole area. Speyside itself is a very picturesque fishing village in front of the thickly forested slopes of the island's Main Ridge. Jemma's Sea View Kitchen and its tree-house restaurant above the sea makes for a very pleasant lunch stop. Reservations can be made in advance (tel: 660 4066).

Villagers are usually eager to offer boat trips to **Little Tobago** (or Goat Island) 1km off shore, and one of the foremost bird sanctuaries in the Caribbean. It was here Sir William Ingram introduced the fabulous Bird of Paradise from New Guinea. However, despite what some islanders might say, it seems there are none left. Reef tours by glass-bottomed boat are also popular and the snorkelling is excellent.

5 CHARLOTTEVILLE

Between Speyside and Charlotteville, the Windward Road becomes a winding roller coaster through a garden of thick tropical vegetation. Near the top of the hill, just before Charlotteville, a hair-raising stretch of road leads to a lookout point and lighthouse with a fine view over Tobago's north coast. The fishing community of Charlotteville gathers itself round Man o'War Bay, its colourful houses clinging to their different pitches on the hillside. There are good bathing beaches near by and a nature trail follows a rough track to a flight of 100 steps and a lookout point at what is thought to have once been a pirate's hideout.

There has been talk for years of an improved road across the top of the island. If it has been built, take it and complete a circle by way of the Caribbean coast; if not return by the Windward Road again.

Houses on stilts among the trees above Charlotteville

LANGUAGE

To be told that the official language of, say, St Lucia is English or that the main tongue of Saba is Dutch, or that they speak French on Les Saintes is to hear only part of the story. Most of the people in the Caribbean speak a local dialect which

The Caribbean is a melting-pot of languages, the result of the colonial power struggle – the island of St Martin/ St Maarten is an extreme example

has evolved over the years from different cultures and nationalities. For example there are still words used on several of the islands which can be traced back to the original Amerindians who migrated from South America. Other phrases and words stem directly from the west of Africa and came over with the slaves.

The struggle between the colonial powers is also reflected in the language. The Creole dialect of St Lucia, an island which was ultimately British, borrows most of its words from the French. And the patois of St Maarten contains elements from Dutch, French, English and Spanish, while the US Virgin Islands throw in a sprinkling of Danish as well.

Even when the language is mostly English or French, there is no guarantee it will be understood by other native English or French speakers when delivered at normal speed; words are often clipped, sometimes they are missed out completely, sometimes they have changed their meaning, sometimes the pronunciation of key syllables is changed. Antiguan English, for example, often replaces 'th' with 't' or 'd'. It gets even more complicated when the patois actually differs from one side of the island to the other, as it does on St Barthélemy, where the Creole on the windwardside is different from the leeward.

Most islands have a phrase book on sale; buy it, teach yourself the local lingo then try it out on the market traders on a Saturday morning. It might not get you a better price for bananas, but it will please the islanders. And everybody understands a smile.

GETTING AWAY FROM IT ALL

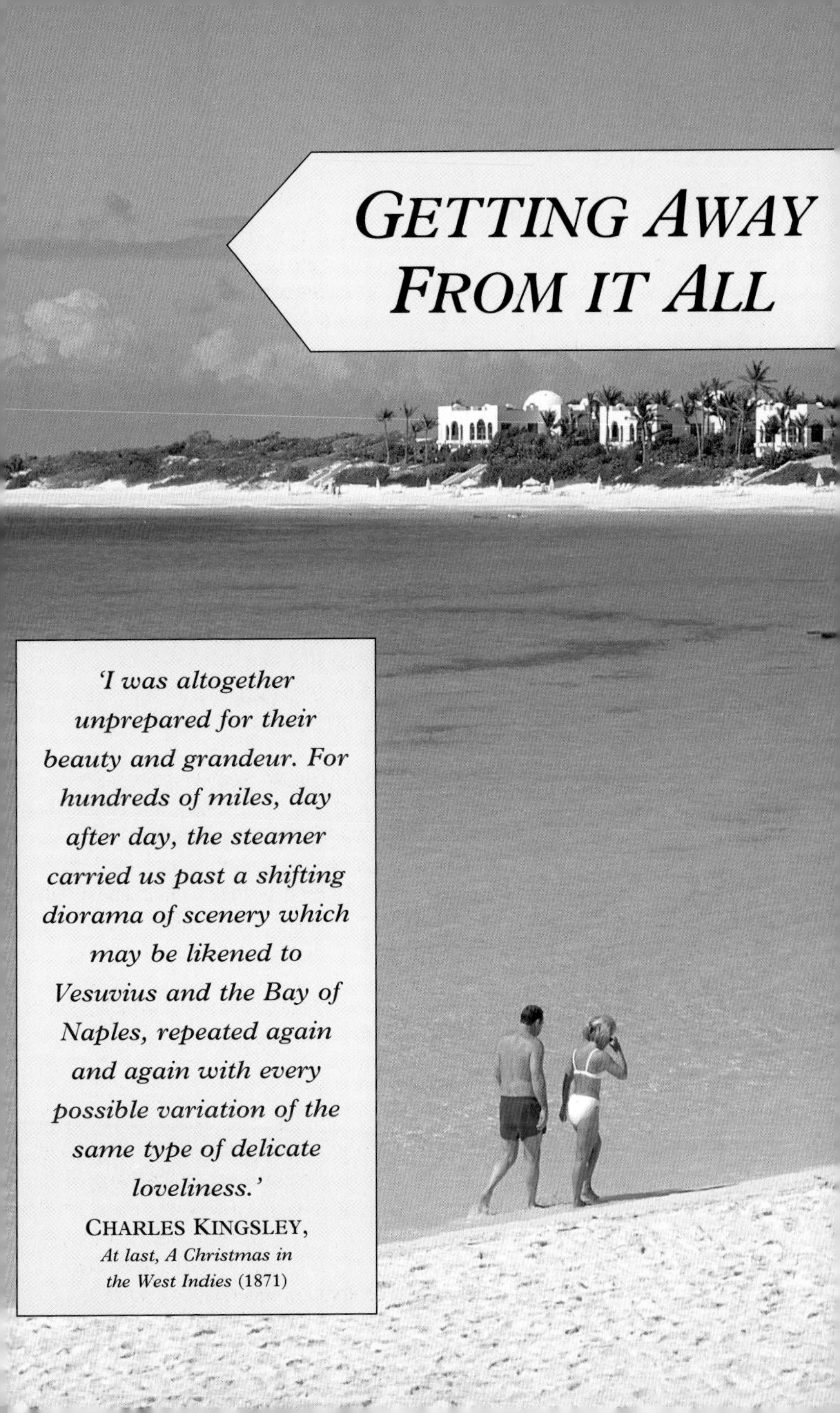

'I was altogether unprepared for their beauty and grandeur. For hundreds of miles, day after day, the steamer carried us past a shifting diorama of scenery which may be likened to Vesuvius and the Bay of Naples, repeated again and again with every possible variation of the same type of delicate loveliness.'

CHARLES KINGSLEY,
At last, A Christmas in the West Indies (1871)

BOAT TRIPS

When the beach seems too crowded or the town is bursting at the seams, the time has come for a boat trip.

There are many ways to take to the waters around the Caribbean. Sometimes it is simply enough to enjoy a ferry ride to another, perhaps smaller, island close at hand. Alternatively, there may be organised boat trips to take you to your own deserted coral atoll for a day of snorkelling, swimming and leaving Robinson Crusoe footsteps on the empty sands.

Other skippers offer a day or half-day cruise around the island or along the coast, usually with lunch provided and often with as much rum punch as you can drink. Some are timed to coincide with sunset, which can be glorious in itself.

Island tourist offices (see page 189) should have a comprehensive list of boat trips and their prices, but the following are recommended.

Anguilla

There is a regular water taxi service (*tel: 497 6395*) plying the 3km between Sandy Ground and little Sandy Island, with its nine palm trees and a beach bar. The sand is good and the snorkelling is excellent; if too many other people have had the same idea, try Scilly Cay or take the ferry to Prickly Pear.

Antigua

Anyone who wonders what it used to be like to walk the plank, might enjoy a Jolly Roger fun cruise, complete with pirate crew (*tel: 462 2064*). Several island skippers offer day cruises to Bird Island and Barbuda; another leaves Hodges Bay for the five-minute trip to Prickly Pear Island; some offer snorkelling expeditions.

Antigua's Jolly Roger cruise

Barbados
Another 'Jolly Roger' (*tel: 436 6424*) sets sail daily from Bridgetown for a lunch and rum punch party, while the *Bajan Queen* (*tel: 436 2149*) offers Carnival night-time cruises.

Grenada
The *Rhum Runner* (*tel: 440 2198*) stops at beaches for sunbathing and reefs for snorkelling, and offers drinks and dancing on board. Captain Peters' Water Taxis (*tel: 440 1349*) make daily trips to little Calivigny and Hog Islands, and to Sandy Island on Tuesdays and Fridays for snorkelling and barbecues featuring local food.

Guadeloupe
Water taxis regularly cross to Ilet du Gosier from Gosier for secluded sunbathing, while larger ferries travel to Marie-Galante and Les Saintes. A glass-bottomed catamaran called *Papyrus* (*tel: 90 92 98*) has day sails with rum and dancing.

Martinique
The Affaires Maritimes (*tel: 71 90 05*) has details of island sailing, snorkelling and beach trips. The Aquarium (*tel: 61 49 49*) is a glass-bottomed boat offering excursions.

St Kitts
Several yachts, such as the *Spirit of St Kitts* (*tel: 465 7474*) and *Tropical Dreamer* (*tel: 465 8224*) offer day sails around the islands with picnic and snorkelling equipment included. Kantours (*tel: 465 2098*) has a Banana Bay beach safari with an evening barbecue.

St Lucia
The *Brig Unicorn* (*tel: 452 6811*), which was used in the filming of the television programme *Roots*, sails down the west coast of the island to Soufrière with a buffet lunch and plenty of rum on board.

Avast there! Landlubbers aboard a Jolly Roger fun cruise

The catamaran *Endless Summer* (*tel: 452 8651*) and the trimaran *Surf Queen* (*tel: 452 8351*) offer similar trips and include a chance to stop for snorkelling and swimming.

St Maarten/St Martin
A whole fleet of yachts set sail daily for smaller islands near by, such as *Bluebeard II* (*tel: 542801*), which sails to Anguilla and Prickly Pear Island. The catamaran *White Octopus* (*tel: 523170*) has popular full-moon and cocktail cruises.

St Vincent and the Grenadines
The perfect escape from St Vincent is to the Grenadines (ferries run regularly from Kingstown to Bequia). Once there, numerous smaller boats are available to take you to deserted beaches or sandy islands such as the Tobago Cays.

Virgin Islands, British and US
There are so many little islands in the group and so many yachts ready and willing to take you there it is hard to know where to begin. Calypso Boats (*tel: 775 2628*) on St Thomas hire out power boats by the hour, while Big Beard's Adventure Tours (*tel: 773 44820*) offers trips to Buck Island.

CRUISING THE CARIBBEAN

Cruising is still considered the ultimate luxury holiday and the Caribbean is the world's number one cruise ship destination. However, this popularity has led to an embarrassment of riches. There are something like 150 cruise ships visiting Caribbean islands every year and a choice of vessel which ranges from 2,000-passenger monsters to a small four-masted sailing schooner and a list of destinations covering every island in this book.

Listed here are some of the most popular cruise lines visiting the region. The addresses and telephone numbers refer to the head office of each company, but of course their cruises are sold by travel agents throughout the world.

Carnival Cruise Lines, one of the fastest-growing cruise companies in the world, run at least nine ships in the Caribbean. Their style is youthful and very informal with an emphasis on action-packed fun. Because of the size of their ships, they tend to visit the largest islands in the group.
3655 NW 78th Avenue, Miami, FL 33178, USA (tel: 0101 305 599 2600).

Celebrity Cruises have three large ships providing a fairly luxurious service at moderate prices. They visit Antigua, Barbados, Martinique, St Lucia, St Maarten/St Martin and the Virgin Islands.
900 Third Avenue, New York, NY 10022, USA (tel: 0101 800 437 3111).

Club Méditerrané's two ships are imbued with the same French ambience as their famous holiday resorts. The atmosphere on board is distinctly casual with sports and activities to the fore. They are wind assisted and being of moderate size they manage to visit smaller ports such as Bequia, Virgin Gorda, St Kitts and Tobago.
40 West 57th Street, New York NY 10019, USA (tel: 0101 212 977 2100).

Costa Cruise Lines is another big player in the region with at least nine ships offering what they call 'cruising Italian style'. They visit ports such as St

The big cruise ships change the look, and fortunes, of many of these islands

Choose from sail boats and cruise ships

Lucia, Antigua and Tortola.
5 Casa Postale, 492 1-16121 Genoa, Italy (tel: 010 54831).

Cunard is perhaps the most famous name in cruising and is well represented in the Caribbean with several large modern ships offering a very high standard of comfort and on-board facilities. Again, the ports visited tend to be among the larger in the area, such as Martinique, Grenada and Antigua.
Canute Road, Southampton SO1, UK (tel: 0703 229933).

Norwegian Cruise Line boasts several popular and affordable cruise ships including the *Norway*, at 2,000 passengers one of the biggest sailing in the region. While the smaller ships call in at Antigua and Barbados, the Norway sticks to the big shopping destinations, St Thomas and St Maarten/St Martin.
Two Alhambra Plaza, Coral Gables, FL 33134, USA (tel: 0101 305 447 9660).

Princess Cruises are right in the mainstream of Caribbean cruising with at least 10, modern, sleek liners offering a range of cruises which prove particularly popular with the older age group.
77 New Oxford Street, London WC1A 1PP UK (tel: 071 831 1881).

Renaissance Cruises have several small, very luxurious ships which appeal to wealthy and more adventurous cruisers. There are usually lectures on board and the ships visit small ports such as Virgin Gorda and Anguilla.
1800 Eller Drive, Suite 300, Fort Lauderdale, FL 7316, USA (tel: 0101 305 463 0982).

Royal Caribbean Cruise Line is dedicated to year-round Caribbean cruising with a fleet of modern ships which appeal to a wide range of people. St Thomas and St Maarten/St Martin are popular destinations.
1050 Caribbean Way, Miami, FL 33132, USA (tel: 0101 305 539 6000).

Star Clipper offers perhaps the best small cruise ship experience of them all, with two specially commissioned, four-masted schooners sailing under 35,000 sq m of sail and visiting small ports such as the Saintes, St Barthélemy and Nevis.
143 Avenue Molière, 1060 Brussels, Belgium (tel: 010 322 347 3435).
Windstar Cruises operates three 'sailcruisers'; sleek, computer-controlled, wind assisted cruise ships calling in at places such as Tortola, Bequia and St Barthélemy.
300 Elliott Avenue West, Seattle, WA 98119 (tel: 0101 206 281 3535).

PRIVATE YACHT CHARTERS

For many people, the most enjoyable way to cruise the Caribbean is on a boat of their own – even if they have to give it back at the end of the week.

There are many different kinds to choose from, ranging from the fast and sleek to the slow and stately; but the first choice to be made is between crewed and 'bareboat' vessels. Crewed yachts usually have a skipper and a mate who will sail, navigate the boat and cook. 'Bareboats' offer more independence but are only for experienced sailors.

Most of the charter boat companies are based on Antigua, Grenada, Guadeloupe, Martinique, St Lucia, St Maarten/St Martin, St Vincent and the Grenadines and – particularly – the Virgin Islands, both British and US. Local tourist offices (see page 189) or specialist yacht magazines can supply addresses.

BANANA BOATS

One of the most interesting ways to cruise the Caribbean is from Europe on a banana boat, or at least one of the modern cargo ships which make the journey every month from France or Britain. The food is good, the life is peaceful and it offers a different view of life at sea. Try the Geest Line, Barry Docks, South Glamorgan, Wales, UK (tel: 0446 700333).

Luxury yachts moored at Nelson's dockyard on Antigua

DIRECTORY

'These green slopes, hemmed in by their Garden of Eden forests, have an almost miraculous beauty. In the extending shadows of the late-afternoon sunlight they appear as idyllic and eternal as the clearings in a rather sad heaven.'

PATRICK LEIGH FERMOR

(1951)

Shopping

*F*rom a simple hand-made basket in a market to a diamond bracelet in a top quality duty-free store, the Caribbean has everything to satisfy even the most addicted shopaholic. The secret is to know what to buy – and where to get it. Shopping hours vary not only between islands but also from shop to shop within the same island. Some have lunch hours, some do not; some open late in the evening, others have variable half days. Be patient.

ANGUILLA
Artwork and island clothes are this island's specialities. Several local artists sell their work in galleries throughout the island. Look particularly for the paintings of Michèle Lavalette, Iris Lewis, Roland Richardson and David Hodges. Irene Edwards of Sandy Ground makes very fine embroidery, Cheddie from Cove specialises in driftwood sculptures, while the Anguilla Arts and Crafts Centre in The Valley (*tel: 497 3200*) has a good general selection.

Caribbean Silk Screen (*tel: 497 2272*) boasts a range of colourful clothing, as does the Sunshine Shop (*tel: 497 2149*) in South Hill. Lismaca Boutique in The Valley (no phone) has locally designed dresses.

Thousands of wayside stalls make a modest living from the tourist trade

ANTIGUA
Heritage Quay by the cruise ship dock in St John's is popular for international duty free items. Redcliffe Quay has more local shops in its beautifully restored waterfront buildings, such as Things Caribbean (*tel: 462 4219*) with colourful beachwear and tie-dyed shirts, A Thousand Flowers (*tel: 462 4264*) which sells only items made from natural fibres and Karibbean Kids (*tel: 462 4566*) with gifts for children.

Antigua's best-known arts and crafts outlet is Harmony Hall (*tel: 460 4120*) at Brown's Bay where there are regular displays of paintings for sale as well as ceramics, scupltures, books and cards.

BARBADOS
Bridgetown has several modern shopping centres, particularly in Broad Street, where there is an array of luxury goods for sale, some at duty-free prices. With its long and settled history, Barbados is especially attractive to those seeking older merchandise. There are several antique shops on the island, such as Antiquaria (*tel: 426 0635*) near the cathedral, and Greenwich House Antiques (*tel: 432 1169*) in Greenwich Village. The Best of Barbados (*tel: 436 1416*), a mini-chain of shops around the island, has some excellent locally made craftwork while Origins (*tel: 436 8522*) specialises in hand-painted clothes.

Part of Heritage Quay shopping area, Antigua

DOMINICA

Here you can find some of the best basketry in the region, woven in traditional patterns by the descendants of the Carib Indians. Their distinctive two-tone handiwork is on sale throughout the island. Tropicrafts (*tel: 448 7126*) in Roseau sells it, along with baskets of island spices, Dominica Bay Rum and coconut oil soap. Also in Roseau, Arnold and Roberta Toulon (*tel: 448 3740*) sell hand-painted T-shirts, while The Old Mill culture centre on Canefield Road sells top-quality local wood carvings.

GRENADA

Few people return home from Grenada without at least one little basket of island spices. While these make very attractive gifts, they are cheaper when assembled separately from the produce at St George's market. Spice Island Perfumes (*tel: 440 2006*) on the Carenage and Arawak Islands (*tel: 440 4577*) in Upper Belmont Road also sell perfumes and colognes made from exotic island plants. Creation Arts and Crafts (*tel: 440 0570*) in St George's sells jewellery and hand-painted clothes while Gifts Remembered (*tel: 440 2482*) has some well-made handicrafts.

The paintings of the artist Canute Calliste are on sale at his studio on Carriacou.

MARKETS

Vibrant, colourful, exciting, noisy; one of the highlights of a trip to town has to be a visit to the local market. Every town has one and it is usually at its busiest on a Saturday morning. But beware: it starts early before the day heats up, so the earlier you get there, the more there is to see.

The scene can be thoroughly confusing. The stalls and the streets around the market are often crowded, haphazardly filled

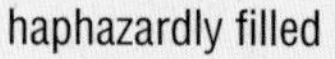

with brightly dressed islanders beneath broad colourful umbrellas, with various arrangements of strange-looking fruits and vegetables piled at their feet. Some customers move quietly and purposefully, picking up the best of the displayed produce, examining it, moving on to compare; others negotiate noisily in the local patois with sweeping gestures and

Caribbean markets
Below: St George's, Grenada
Bottom left: Marigot, French St Martin
Centre left: Forte-de-France, Martinique

appeals.

Much of the produce will be familiar from supermarket displays, but often with subtle differences. Everybody knows what a banana looks like, for example, but only a few of the many varieties grown in the Caribbean are exported to Europe or North America. Here, then, is a chance to try some different types – vendors are always willing to explain anything unfamiliar. The small collection of fruit or vegetables at a vendor's feet is usually arranged in the quantity it is sold in, for a set amount of money; say three oranges or a soursop for two dollars. Visitors are seldom expected to haggle – a few bananas are unlikely to be beyond the purse of a holiday-maker anyway.

GUADELOUPE

Pointe-à-Pitre is one place where it pays to carry travellers' cheques, for many of the best shops in the city offer a 20 per cent discount when goods are paid for in this way. As well as stores stocking upmarket goods from mainland France, there are plenty of outlets for good local products – such as straw baskets, traditional hats, Madras tablecloths and, of course, bottles of rum. For island antiques, try Tim Tim (*tel: 83 48 71*) in Rue Henri IV or L'Imagerie Creole (*tel: 90 87 28*) at Bras-du-Fort.

MARTINIQUE

Fort-de-France is famous for its mix of chic and tropical shops; so it is good to know that the same 20 per cent travellers' cheque discount applies here as in Guadeloupe. The latest Paris fashions can be found in the shops in the centre of town together with some brilliantly original clothes designed on the island. More down-to-earth, but none-the-less worthy, island handicrafts can be found at the Caribbean Art Centre (*tel: 70 32 16*) near the tourist office.

MONTSERRAT

Whatever the brochures may say, Plymouth is not really a Mecca for shoppers, but there are a few shops selling quality artwork, and prints of island scenes make good souvenirs. These are best bought unframed and then framed at home. The Island House Art Gallery (*tel: 491 3938*) in John Street is the best place to browse. Just Looking (*tel: 491 4076*) near by also has hand-painted fabrics and batiks, while the Tapestries of Montserrat (*tel: 491 2520*) in Parliament Street has some beautiful hand-crafted rugs and wallhangings.

Handicrafts stall in a Carib Indian reservation on Dominica

NEVIS

There are several outlets for hand-crafted goods on Nevis, including Made in Nevis beside the museum at Alexander Hamilton's birthplace where they sell Creole pottery, baskets and jewellery, and Nevis Handicraft Co-op (*tel: 469 5509*), where you find locally made clothing, woven goods, jams and jellies. Nevis Products at Highlands House in Charlestown incorporates prints by local artists on to coasters and placemats.

SABA

The island's best-known products are its hand-embroidered lace and Saba spice, a home-made liqueur. Both can be bought readily in shops throughout the island.

ST BARTHELEMY

Gustavia is a duty-free port but the luxury goods displayed in its stores are still very expensive. The village of Corossol near by is famous for its intricate straw-work. Bags, baskets and hats can all be bought from the women working at the roadside.

ST EUSTATIUS

There may not be much to take home from St Eustatius but local artwork is usually on sale at the Park Place Gallery (*tel: 382452*) in Oranjestad. The Hole in the Wall (*tel: 382265*) near by has hand-painted clothes.

ST KITTS

Basseterre has a good new shopping centre, The Pelican Mall, on the waterfront, with clothing and gifts designed on the island, as well as duty-free items. Caribelle Batik (*tel: 465 6253*) is a famously picturesque shopping stop at Romney Manor where they sell hand-printed shirts and dresses.

Souvenirs can range from rum, to antiques, to colourful dolls such as these on Martinique

ST LUCIA

The most popular source of duty-free shopping on the island is in the modern complex at Pointe Seraphine outside Castries. Here, and at other locations, Bagshaw Studios (*tel: 452 7570*) and Windjammer Clothing (*tel: 452 2139*) sell top-quality colourful silk screen fabrics and clothing. A Touch of Class (*tel: 452 3817*) also at Pointe Seraphine is good for local souvenirs, while other colourful Caribbean gifts, such as miniature steel pans and handcrafted dolls, can be found at Noah's Arcade (*tel: 452 2523*). Although they may be heavy to carry home, authentic clay cooking pots make interesting souvenirs from the Castries market in Jeremie Street.

Wooden crafts for many occasions on Dutch St Maarten

ST MAARTEN/ST MARTIN

Philipsburg's Front Street is crammed every day with cruise ship passengers looking for duty-free bargains. European items are particularly treasured by the American visitors, less so by Europeans. Numerous shops advertise electronic goods at bargain prices, but it is best to check prices at home first before shopping. There are several modern shopping complexes specialising in watches, gold and jewellery, and T-shirt shops abound. The Shipwreck Shop near the central jetty has some locally-made jewellery as well as island artwork. Marigot is marginally less frantic and here the visitor finds French fashions flown in from Paris. Duty-free liquor is cheap in both towns and includes the island's own Guavaberry liqueur.

ST VINCENT AND THE GRENADINES

Kingstown has few good-quality shops; islanders tend to peddle second-rate carvings on the streets. However, the St Vincent Craftsmen Centre (*tel: 457 1288*) sells colourful baskets, place mats, bamboo lampshades and unusual floor mats made from plaited lavender. Look also for the distinctive Banana Art by Ras Randy Payne who works with the bark and leaves of the banana plant. Noah's Arkade (*tel: 458 3424*) has more conventional souvenirs including baskets of spices, carvings and books.

The most sought-after souvenir in the Grenadines is a hand-made model boat from Bequia. Craftsmen in shops along the bay in Port Elizabeth carve replicas of famous sailing ships, yachts or just traditional Bequia whale boats. A specially commissioned custom-made boat can take several weeks and tends to be very expensive. The other main industry in Bequia is in hand-painted clothes.

TOBAGO

Apart from hotel boutiques, most of the shops are to be found in Lower Scarborough Mall, in the new cruise ship complex and in the street market near by. However, the Cotton House (*tel: 639 3695*) has some good batik and jewellery while The Hangover Art Gallery (*tel: 639 7940*) at Pigeon Point sells local artwork.

TRINIDAD

The best buys are those which reflect the colourful side of Trinidad's carnival character. Tapes and records of favourite Calypsonians make evocative souvenirs and can be bought at Rhyner's (*tel: 623 5673*) in Port of Spain. Several stores at the south end of Frederick Street sell brilliantly printed fabrics reflecting the island's Indian heritage. Local art work and handicrafts can be found at the Village (*tel: 624 1181*) in Nook Avenue and Art Creators (*tel: 624 4369*) in St Ann's Road.

VIRGIN ISLANDS, BRITISH

The best shopping area in Road Town is in the Main Street behind Pusser's bar. Bonker's Gallery (*tel: 494 2535*) has original dresses and sarongs, Flaxcraft Jewellery (*tel: 494 2892*) sells interesting pieces using island shells and the Shipwreck Shop (*tel: 494 2567*) has baskets, hammocks and coral jewellery. At the west end of the island, Soper's Hole has several modern shops including Sea Urchin (*tel: 494 3129*) and Collector's Corner (*tel: 494 3550*).

VIRGIN ISLANDS, US

Cruise ship passengers go crazy when they hit the streets of Charlotte Amalie, where the duty-free goods include gold and jewellery, watches, china and alcohol. Competition between the stores is fierce and it is worth bargaining a little if an item, such as a popular make of watch, is available in several different stores.

Paintings and prints can be found at The Gallery (*tel: 776 4641*) in Veteran's Drive and the Caribbean Art Print Gallery (*tel: 776 2303*) in Riise's Alley, while Local Color (*tel: 774 3727*) also has clothing and jewellery designed on the island.

On St Croix, Crucian Gold (*tel: 773 5241*) and Sonya's (*tel: 778 8605*) in Christiansted both sell highly original jewellery, while Collage (*tel: 773 0066*) features the work of Crucian artists.

The tourist market in Marigot, French St Martin

Entertainment

It is when the sun goes down that the fun really starts in the Caribbean; there are street parties, barbecue nights, discos, limbo competitions, crab races, calypso contests and impromptu parties (known as jump-ups) nearly every night somewhere on every island. Occasionally there are cultural nights, when a dance troupe or group of island singers re-create an earlier age, perhaps the days of slavery on the sugar plantations; anyone supporting one of these is helping to preserve the island's heritage.

There are several first-class free publications available at island tourist offices listing events and most hotel concierges can tell you what's on, where.

The liveliest parties are often 'Island Nights' when local food is prepared, usually buffet style, and a band, sometimes a steel band, arrives to play some authentic island music. Beware, there may be fun and games. One of the the most popular is limbo dancing and crab races, which involve small bets, also cause great amusement.

The same show tends to do the rounds of several hotels on the island so anyone who misses an Island Night in their own hotel need only enquire of the tourist office to find out where they can catch it the next evening. Here are a few more, equally entertaining, possibilities:

ANGUILLA

La Sirena

Features performances every Thursday by the Mayoumba Folkloric Group, dancing and singing about Caribbean life (*tel: 497 6827*).

The Cinnamon Reef Resort

Has nightly entertainment with music and a lively Friday night barbecue (*tel: 497 2850*).

Johnno's Beach Bar

Offers outdoor dancing at weekends. *Sandy Ground* (*tel: 497 2728*).

The Coconut Paradise

Has nightly entertainment and frequent limbo sessions. *Island Harbour* (*tel: 497 4454*).

ANTIGUA

Tropix

This is a popular disco open Wednesday to Saturday. *Redcliffe Quay, St John's* (*tel: 462 2317*).

Columbo's

Specialises in live reggae. *English Harbour* (*tel: 463 1081*).

The Lemon Tree Restaurant

Has dancing every evening after dinner. *Long Street, St John's* (*tel: 461 2507*).

King's Casino

Suits anyone who enjoys a little flutter. *Heritage Quay, St John's* (*tel: 462 1727*).

BARBADOS

The Plantation Tropical Spectacular

This is a Monday night entertainment featuring a steel band, limbo dancers and fire eaters. *St Lawrence Road, Bridgetown* (*tel: 428 5048*).

After Dark

A bar with a popular late night jazz club. *St Lawrence Gap, Christ Church* (*tel: 435 6547*).

1627 And All That

A celebrated show featuring island folklore. *Barbados Museum, Highway 7* (*tel: 435 6900*).

Plantation Tropical Spectacular, Barbados

Harbour Lights
Has live music and dancing nearly every night. *Bay Street, St Michael (tel: 436 7225).*
Baxter Road, Bridgetown, is famous for its late night food vendors and local rum.

DOMINICA
Wykie's Tropical Bar
Lively, particularly on Friday nights when a local calypso or string band plays. *Old Street, Roseau (tel: 448 8015).*
The Shipwreck
Has live reggae at weekends. *Canefield (tel: 449 1059).*
The Warehouse
A popular local disco. *Roseau (tel: 449 1303).*

GRENADA
Dynamite Disco
Usually crowded with islanders. *Grand Anse (tel: 444 4056).*
The Marryshow Theatre
Features concerts, plays and special events. *Tyrrel Street, St George's.*
The Boatyard Bar
Has dancing after dinner on Wednesdays and a steel band until late on Fridays. *Lance aux Epines.*
Fantazia 2001
Good mixture of local and international dance music. *Morne Beach (tel: 444 4224).*

GUADELOUPE
Le Jardin Bresilien
Often has live music on its terrace. *Bras-du-Fort (tel: 90 99 31).*
Le Foufou
A lively, but pricey disco. *Bras-du-Fort (tel:84 35 59).*
Cornel's Piano Bar
Has a jazz band at weekends. *Rue Intermediaire Assainissement, Pointe-à-Pitre.*
Casino de Gosier Les Bains
A complex consisting of a popular restaurant, bar and nightclub. *Pointe de la Verdure (tel: 84 18 33).*

MARTINIQUE

Les Grands Ballets de Martinique
One of the best-known folkloric groups in the region. *Various venues (tel: 63 43 88)*.

Le New Hippo
A fashionable disco. *Boulevard Allegre, Fort-de-France (tel:71 74 60)*.

The Neptune
A good place to hear zouk music. *Diamant (tel: 76 34 23)*.

The Casino Trois-Ilets
A relaxed casino for the over-21s. *Meridien Hotel (tel: 66 00 00)*.

Limbo with fire, St Lucia

MONTSERRAT

Vue Pointe Hotel
Has a lively Wednesday night barbecue with steel band music. *Vue Pointe (tel: 491 5210)*.

Nepcoden
Attracts crowds for its rotis and dancing. *Weekes (no phone)*.

The Yacht Club
Comes to life on Friday nights. *Wapping (tel: 491 2237)*.

NEVIS

Golden Rock Estate
Has an authentic island string band accompanying the Saturday night barbecue. *Gingerland (tel: 469 3346)*.

Croney's Old Manor Estate
Has a buffet on Friday nights accompanied by steel band music. *Charlestown (tel: 469 3445)*.

SABA

The Lime Tree Bar
One of the hottest places in town. *The Bottom (tel: 463 256)*.

Guido's Pizzaria
Turns itself into a disco on Saturday nights. *Windwardside (tel: 462 330)*.

ST BARTHÉLEMY

Autour du Rocher
A disco for late night dancing. *Lorient (tel: 27 60 73)*.

Le Pelican
A more restrained piano bar. *St Jean Beach (tel: 27 64 64)*.

ST EUSTATIUS

Talk of the Town
Has a lively music party on Friday nights. *Saddlerweg (tel: 382236)*.

Cool Corner
Busiest on Saturdays. *Oranjestad (tel: 382523)*.

ST KITTS

The Georgian House
Has live entertainment and a barbecue every Tuesday. *Independence Square, Basseterre (tel: 465 4049).*

Turtle Beach Bar and Grill
Has a Saturday night beach dance and disco. *Turtle Bay (tel:496 9086).*

ST LUCIA

Gros Islet Village
Hosts a huge street party with food and music on Friday nights.

The Green Parrot
Has a floor show with limbo dancers. *Morne Fortune (tel: 452 3399).*

Splash
Has a sophisticated disco. *St Lucian Hotel, (tel: 452 8351).*

The 'A' Pub
Has jazz on a Wednesday night and live dance bands on Friday and Saturday. *Rodney Bay (tel: 452 8725).*

ST VINCENT AND THE GRENADINES

Basil's Too
Has dancing after dinner. *Villa Beach (tel: 458 4205).*

The Attic
Features jazz and steel bands. *Grenville Street, Kingstown (tel: 457 2558).*

Mau Mau Beach Bar
Boasts a popular Saturday party by the sea. *Friendship Bay Hotel, Bequia (tel:458 3222).*

Villa La Bijou
Has a disco at weekends. *Canouan (tel: 458 8025).*

TOBAGO

Sunday School
This is what they call the street party every week at Buccoo village. It goes on until about 4am.

Dancing on Tobago

Karawak Village
Features steel band music and jazz several times a week. *Crown Point (tel: 639 8442).*

TRINIDAD

Mas Camp Pub
Offers a chance to hear top calypsonians in relaxed surroundings. *Ariapata Street, Port of Spain (tel: 627 8449).*

Cricket Wicket
Dance to island sounds here. *Tragarete Road, Port of Spain (tel: 622 1808).*

VIRGIN ISLANDS, BRITISH

Bomba's Shack
Has a riotous Full Moon Party every month. *Long Bay.*

Quito's Gazebo
The place to hear the island singer Quito Rymer. *Cane Garden Bay (tel: 495 4837).*

VIRGIN ISLANDS, US

Barnacle Bill's
Popular with local musicians. *Crown Bay, St Thomas (tel: 774 7444).*

Fred's, Cruz Bay
Has reggae and calypso nights. *St John (tel: 776 6363).*

Calabash
Steel band music Wednesday to Saturday. *Christiansted, St Croix (tel:778 0001).*

CARNIVAL

It has often been said that if the Caribbean islanders put as much energy into developing their economy as they do into preparing for Carnival then the region would be very rich indeed. But where is the fun in that?

Carnival is the biggest event on nearly every island in the Caribbean and most, but not all, celebrate it in the three days before Ash Wednesday (for a list of who celebrates Carnival when see pages 158–9). But preparations generally begin well before that. In fact in Trinidad, where Carnival is almost a national obsession, preparations begin almost as soon as the previous Carnival has finished and pre-Carnival parties get under way as soon as Christmas is past.

Anyone can join in. Most parades are divided into bands, each of which, particularly in Trinidad's case, can number as many as 3,000 celebrants, with their own designers and technicians. The leaders of these bands post the costume designs for each of the different characters in their band well in advance and whoever wants to wear that costume and march with that particular band can pay a deposit and register for a place in the parade.

Two weeks before Carnival, preparations are in full swing; costumes are finished off, sets and floats are built and the calypsonians who will compete for the traditional title of Calypso Monarch of the year are practising frantically and their 'tents', as they are

called, become the focus of lively late night parties. The calypso final usually takes place on Carnival Sunday, Dimanche Gras. As soon as the Monarch is crowned, the celebration really begins and as night slips into Monday morning, J'Ouvert as it is called, the road marches get under way (although this 'marching' is really more a kind of dancing). The grand finale is of course the next day, Mardi Gras, with the procession of the bands and the brightest, most colourful, happiest, noisiest parade the island has seen (since last year).

Festivals and Events

*N*early every island has at least one special time during the year when locals seize the opportunity to dance in the streets, to wear funny hats or simply to celebrate life in the sunshine islands. This a calendar of some of the liveliest events. Exact dates and venues vary from year to year so check with local tourist offices (see page 189).

JANUARY
Antigua: Tennis week – professional tournament and friendly competitions
Barbados: Windsurfing competitions
Grenada: Sailing regatta and Game Fishing tournament
Guadeloupe: Beginning of Carnival
St Barthélemy: Music festival with local and international artists
St Lucia: New Year's Fiesta

FEBRUARY
Barbados: Holetown Festival, celebrating arrival of first British settlers
Guadeloupe, **Martinique**, **St Barthélemy**, **St Lucia**, **St Maarten/St Martin**, **Trinidad** and **Tobago:** Carnival (see pages 156–7)
Grenada: Independence Day celebrations

MARCH
Montserrat: St Patrick's Day on the Emerald Isle
Trinidad: Hindu Pagwah Festival

APRIL
Antigua: Sailing Week – one of the biggest in the world
Barbados: Oistins Fish Festival
Grenada: Easter regatta
Saba, **St Eustatius** and **St Maarten/St Martin:** Parties to celebrate the official birthday of Queen Beatrix
St Vincent and the Grenadines: Bequia's Easter regatta
Virgin Islands, British: Spring Regatta
Virgin Islands, US: Carnival

MAY
Anguilla: Traditional boat racing
Barbados: Caribbean Jazz Festival
St Maarten/St Martin: Food Festival

JUNE
Montserrat: Queen's birthday celebrations
St Lucia: Aqua Festival, with races, competitions and traditional boat decorating
Virgin Islands, British and US: Windsurfing regatta around both sets of islands
Virgin Islands, US: Frenchtown Carnival on St Thomas

JULY
Antigua: Windsurfing Antigua Week
Barbados: Cropover – an exciting month-long celebration at the end of harvest time
Guadeloupe, Martinique: Bastille Day celebrations

St Croix Christmas festival

Martinique: Fort-de-France Festival
Saba: Carnival
St Maarten/St Martin: Boat races to mark Schoelcher Day
Tobago: Tobago Heritage Festival

AUGUST
Anguilla: Carnival
Grenada: Carnival, the Rainbow City Festival and the Carriacou Regatta
Guadeloupe: Festival of Cooks parade and all-day feast
Martinique: Boat races for traditional yawls
Nevis: Culturama Festival
St Barthélemy: Saint's day festival
St Lucia: La Rose Flower Society parade
Trinidad: Santa Rosa Festival in the south

SEPTEMBER
St Barthélemy: Fishing contest and dances in L'Orient
Nevis, St Kitts: Independence celebrations
Trinidad: Muslim Hosein festival
Virgin Islands, US: St John Carnival

OCTOBER
Trinidad: Hindu Festival of Lights
Virgin Islands, US: Hurricane Thanksgiving Day

NOVEMBER
Barbados: National Independence Festival of the Creative Arts
Dominica: Independence celebrations
St Eustatius: Statia/America Day celebrating historic friendship
St Maarten/St Martin: Concordia Day celebrating historic friendship
Trinidad: Pan Jazz Festival

DECEMBER
All islands celebrate **Christmas**, but some, notably Montserrat and Tobago, seem to celebrate it even more than Carnival.
Anguilla: Separation Day festivities
Barbados: International road races
Guadeloupe, Martinique, St Barthélemy: Reveillon season celebrations
Guadeloupe: Young Saints' Day children's parade
Nevis, St Kitts: Carnival
St Barthélemy: Transatlantic tall ships regatta and festival
St Lucia: National Day celebration
St Vincent: Nine Mornings festivities leading up to Christmas

Children

There can be little reason for a child to be bored in the Caribbean. Island tourist offices (see page 189) will have listings of local attractions.

SUNNY DAYS

The beach is the most obvious attraction. While Caribbean sand seldom makes good sandcastles, it often makes a useful football pitch or volleyball court. Bring some beach games with you such as beach tennis and a frisbee (and do not forget a high-factor sun screen to prevent sunburn). Small children enjoy collecting the colourful and interesting shells to be found on a few shell beaches in the region.

Some hotels and resorts have children's programmes: they may well come back after a picnic lunch with painted faces or dressed as pirates and are almost certain to have made some new friends.

The sea is usually safe for swimming on the Caribbean coast but children should be watched at all times. There are good opportunities to learn windsurfing, dinghy-sailing or water-skiing. Hire a small boat, or even charter a yacht for a few hours, to give the children a change of scenery or to take them to another beach to try snorkelling. Older children will love the fast motor boats which can be rented for island-hopping, particularly in the Virgin Islands.

There are plenty of riding stables on the islands, but it is important to check they have the right size of pony for your child. Many nature trails and hikes, suitable for smaller legs, offer an introduction to the natural history of an island. Some islands have zoos and aquariums (the emphasis nowadays is on conserving local species) and in St Maarten/St Martin there is a spectacular eagle show held daily at Maho Bay. At Carnival time, particularly in Trinidad, there are usually children's events including their own parade and jump-up, and St Maarten/St Martin has a Fun City where they can learn about limbo dancing and steel bands.

RAINY DAYS

When it rains in the Caribbean it really rains, and most hotels are prepared for this eventuality with a selection of board games, cards and dominoes and occasionally some indoor sports such as

darts and table tennis. Videos of the latest cinema releases are frequently shown during the day (and at night, when the children may not be interested in watching the adults dance).

Outside the hotel, island museums are gradually improving their presentations, moving away from the – often boring – row of artefacts in a glass case to more interesting tableaux showing island life in earlier times.

Caribbean gift shops are full of a range of colourfully illustrated books suitable for the younger members of the family.

TROPICAL WATERS

Children of all ages will enjoy a look at the undersea world either in a glass-bottomed boat or, on Barbados and St Thomas, in a real submarine. Dives on the *Atlantis* usually last 45 minutes and go as far as 48m below the surface.

Atlantis Submarines, Bridgetown, Barbados (tel: 436 8929), and Havensight Mall, St Thomas (tel: 776 5650).

Sport

There is a great variety of sporting activities on offer, both for the enthusiastic participant and the spectator. These are just a few. The local tourist offices (see page 189) will have full details.

BEACHES

A Caribbean beach is more than just a strip of sand to lie on; for many people it is one big playground. An impromptu game of football or cricket may well kick off in the early morning or late afternoon and visitors often join in; but the most popular beach sport is volley-ball. Most resorts have nets set up by the shore and will organise informal games for any guests who want to join in.

Curtley Ambrose bowling

For other people the principal attraction of a beach is as a launching pad into the sea. Swimming is safe in most places on the Caribbean coast of each island; but do check locally that there is no vicious undertow or other underwater hazard.

CRICKET

This has become almost an obsession on the British Caribbean islands and there are few villages which do not boast a team and a cricket square. You may be lucky enough to be able to watch an international test match when a touring team visits one of the larger islands; otherwise an inter-island competition, or even a small local tournament, will give a good idea of the support the game enjoys.

CYCLING

Given that cycling is the main participation sport in France, it is not surprising that it is also very popular in the French Antilles. Bicycles, both racing and mountain bikes, can be hired here, and on many other islands, by those with the stamina to withstand the heat.

DIVING (see page 112).

DOMINOES

The slap of dominoes hitting the table is a common sound on many of the islands; the game is played with a considerable amount of animation and in a fiercely competitive spirit.

FISHING

Deep-sea fishing – often known as big-game fishing or sport fishing – can be organised from most Caribbean islands. Crewed boats can be hired by the hour or by the day from harbours and marinas to go in search of marlin, tuna, wahoo and sailfish. These charters usually include tackle, bait, food and refreshments and, of course, instruction. Some islands insist on the purchase of a fishing licence before a line is cast, but sometimes this is included in the cost of the charter. It is also important to establish at the outset whether any fish caught belong to the boat or to the visitor. For the real enthusiast, fishing tournaments are often held on the larger islands; the local tourist office can supply details of these.

Break for dominoes

GOLF

Few major resorts are built these days without a golf course attached. It is one of the fastest growing activities in the Caribbean; even the smaller islands usually cram in at least a nine-hole course. Most are open to non-members on payment of a green fee; in some hotels golf is included in the guest's package. Usually there is equipment available for hire, professionals on hand for lessons and local caddies to carry the clubs.

Golf course, Mount Irvine, Tobago

WATERSPORTS

A holiday in the Caribbean offers the ideal opportunity to learn a watersport. Every beach resort has a range of equipment and most of the watersports are free to hotel guests – although often a fee is charged for activities involving motor boats.

Windsurfing, or boardsailing, is one of the most popular activities. There are normally staff on hand to teach the basic art of standing up straight, the finer points of navigation and sailing technique. Rescue boats will be at the ready.

Water-skiing is also hugely popular and a circuit of the bay may well be offered free of charge to hotel guests. Alternatively, some resorts offer rides on large yellow banana-like inflatables which offer some of the thrills of water-skiing without the need to be able to stand up.

Jet skis have proliferated in the region in recent years and can be fun when the sea is not too crowded. However, they are now banned by some islands because of the noise and nuisance. Sailing a Hobi-Cat is much more peaceful and, again, instructors will be on hand. Perhaps the most leisurely way to take to the water and still enjoy the sun is on a good old-fashioned pedalo.

HIKING
There is excellent walking on all the bigger Caribbean islands, often along the old trails which were used before the roads were built. The local tourist office should be able to mark suitable routes on a map as well as supply information on organised hikes in the area. Guided walks are sometimes arranged through rainforests, national parks or even through city streets, led by a nature conservancy or national trust. Strong shoes are advisable and, if walking independently, leave a note of your intended route with the hotel reception or police. The best time of day is from dawn until about 9.30am and from 4pm to dusk (allowing enough time to return before darkness).

HORSE RACING
The sport of kings is followed fanatically on several of the islands, although race meetings are few and far between. The best-known courses are at the Garrison Savannah in Barbados and the Queens Park Savannah in Trinidad. Polo is also played in Barbados.

HORSE RIDING
This can be a good way to explore off the road and away from the crowds. There are stables on many of the islands; most offer escorted tours, taking in the main sights in one small area, stopping for a picnic lunch and maybe a swim along the way. For the more experienced rider an evening canter along the beach may well be a highlight of the holiday. Tourist offices have a list of stables; check hard hats are supplied.

JOGGING
Many holidaymakers like to go for a run in the late afternoon. If the idea of running solo on an unfamiliar road does not appeal, you can join one of the organised running groups round the islands. The emphasis tends to be on the fun of running rather than the competitive element, although there are also organised road races throughout the region.

KEEP FIT
There are well-equipped gyms open to the public in most Caribbean towns and in the evening it is very common to hear the sounds of an aerobics or jazz exercise class reverberating around the block. On some islands there are yoga classes and therapeutic massage is quite common, even, occasionally, on the beach.

PARASAILING
The idea of dangling by a parachute about 100m above the sea while being pulled along by a motor boat may not appeal to everyone, but the sport of parasailing is becoming increasingly popular in the Caribbean. It is usually available at the island's busiest beaches or larger resorts and can be costly. Check your holiday insurance covers this sort of activity.

PÉTANQUE
There are few towns or stretches of coastline in the French Antilles where a patch of ground has not been cleared for a game of pétanque or boules. It is as relaxing as a spectator sport as it is to play and it is particularly popular in the late afternoon.

RUGBY
Despite the heat, 15-a-side rugby is played on many of the islands with a British connection, such as Barbados and the British Virgin Islands.

Parasailing combines speed, water and flight, and is a growing sport in the Caribbean

TENNIS

Almost every resort in the region has at least one tennis court and often it will be floodlit to allow play in the cool of the evening. The concierge or hotel activities desk will operate a booking system and usually they will specify the dress required on the court. Sometimes guests are expected to provide their own tennis balls (in which case, it is always cheaper to bring them from home than buy them at the hotel).

ANYONE FOR ROAD TENNIS?

A cross between lawn tennis and table tennis, road tennis is very popular in Barbados, Trinidad, St Lucia, St Kitts and Antigua. A strip of wood is placed across the road in place of a net and rackets are carved out of flat pieces of wood. The rules are more like table tennis than its bigger brother and the principal drawback is that play is forced to stop every time a car comes round the corner.

Food and Drink

*F*rom a simple snack at a roadside stand in Trinidad to a four-course formal dinner in Charlotte Amalie, nothing reflects the cultural diversity of the eastern Caribbean as much as its food and drink. There are influences from Africa, India, China, France, Britain, Denmark, Spain, South America and the United States. Every island has its specialities and, for a true taste of the Caribbean, it is worth finding out what these are.

No trip to **Barbados**, for example, would be complete without trying the famous flying fish or the pepperpot, a spicy island stew. There is also *cou-cou*, a dish made of cornmeal and okra that harks back to the slaves from Africa.

Tobago's cooking also remembers its African roots, particularly during the annual Heritage Festival, with dishes such as goat and dumplings and fish cooked with coconut – prepared in traditional iron pots and cooked slowly over wood and coconut-shell fires.

Trinidadians are passionate about their food, particularly the Indian influenced snacks, such as *rotis* (curries wrapped in chapati envelopes) or *doubles* (yellow wheat flour doughs sandwiching a spicy chick pea sauce) or *pelau* (peas and rice, cooked with meat and flavoured with coconut and pepper).

Islands like **St Lucia**, **Dominica** and **Grenada** are renowned for their fresh market produce – although you would not believe it to look at the menus in many of the larger hotels. Unfortunately, when it comes to buying in bulk, hotels often resort to flying in goods from the USA; so, although there may be 22 varieties of fresh fish swimming in the sea around the island, the hotel menu says 'steak'.

On these islands it is worth escaping from the hotel once or twice to try some of the local fruit and vegetables. Look out for some of the staples of the Caribbean diet, eddoes, plantain and breadfruit and, on the French islands, christophenes. Okra and the spinach-like callaloo are often found in traditional African-influenced dishes. Exotic fruits, depending on the season, include papaya, mango, guava, sugar apple (remember to spit out the pips) and, of course, pineapples plus all the diffferent varieties of banana. And you can be sure there will be some island spices to liven things up.

Perhaps the highest standard of

cooking, however, is to be found on the French islands, where food is taken as seriously as it is on the mainland of France. Creole specialities given the French touch include *accras* (sea food fritters often served with a spicy sauce), *court bouillon* (fish in a stock with tomatoes and herbs) and *fricassee de lambis* (conch stew).

DRINK

Cocktails round the pool make a perfect end to an afternoon on the beach and hotels often have 'happy hours', when pre-dinner drinks are available at half the price.

Those wishing to drink wine with their meal will find that, although wine is almost always available in Caribbean restaurants, it is expensive, particularly when imported from Europe.Many people prefer to try island beers instead. As an alternative to coffee, a tisane made with young leaves of the sour orange tree makes a relaxing end to a meal.

HOT SAUCE

No Caribbean dinner table is properly set without a bottle of hot sauce in the middle. It is a tradition which dates back to the Arawak Indians who were known to like pepper juice on their meat. African slaves borrowed the idea to disguise the inferior quality of the food they were given and later the East Indian labourers arrived already with a taste for hot sauce from home. Everyone has their own recipe; some like a red sauce full of tomatoes, others yellow from turmeric and mustard. Look out for Barbados Jack, Erica's Country Style, St Vincent, Pirate Pete's from St Thomas and Matouk's of Trinidad and Tobago. Finally, never pass the hot sauce from hand to hand in Trinidad; it is considered bad luck and breaks the circle of friendship. Always put it down on the table.

WHERE TO EAT

Like just about everything else in the Caribbean, it seems to cost more to dine out during the winter season than it does the rest of the year; but, for a rough guide, the following symbols have been used to indicate the average cost per person, not including alcohol, in some of the best restaurants around the region as listed below.

$ = US$10 or less
$$ = between US$10 and US$20
$$$ = more than US$20

ANGUILLA

The Palm Court $$$
The chefs call it New Caribbean Cuisine. Seaside setting. *Cinnamon Reef Resort, Little Harbour (tel: 2783).*

Koalkeel $$
Local and European in a restored greathouse. *The Valley (tel: 2930).*

Lucy's Harbour View $$
Good local food, recommended by islanders. *Back Street, South Hill (tel: 6253).*

Cap Juluca $$$
Top of the range gourmet fare in an exclusive resort. *Maundays Bay (tel: 6666).*

Imported drinks are expensive, so try Caribbean ones – they are good

ANTIGUA

Brother B's $$
Local food; live music every Saturday. *Long Street, St John's (tel: 462 0616).*

Le Bistro $$$
Celebrated French cuisine in the north end of the island. *Hodges Bay (tel: 462 3881).*

Admiral's Inn $$
A relaxed place for lunch and special-price yachtsman's dinner. *Nelson's Dockyard (tel: 463 1027).*

Shirley Heights Lookout $$
Famous for its Sunday afternoon barbecue and dancing. *Shirley Heights (tel: 460 1785).*

BARBADOS

Pisces $$
Good fish dishes in a waterfront setting. *St Lawrence Gap (tel: 428 6558).*

Granny's $
Traditional local food served by friendly staff. *Oistins village.*

Atlantis Hotel $$$
Celebrated for its Barbados specialities served on a huge Sunday buffet. *Bathsheba (tel: 433 9445).*

DOMINICA

Floral Gardens Hotel $$
Island cooking in a lush tropical setting. *Concord (tel: 57636).*

La Robe Creole $$$
Best-known local food on the island; the staff dress in costume. *Victoria Street, Roseau (tel: 82896).*

GRENADA

Nutmeg $$
Popular island cuisine and famous rum punch overlooking the harbour. *Carenage, St George's (tel: 440 2539).*

Morne Fendue $$
Superb plantation house cooking in a

rural setting. *Morne Fendue (tel: 440 9330).*

GUADELOUPE

Le Karacoli $$
The best of French Creole cuisine by the beach. *Deshaies (tel: 28 41 17).*

Le Château de Feuilles $$$
Barbecued food and their own 25 different kinds of punch. *Anse-Bertrand (tel: 22 30 30).*

Relais du Moulin $$
A successful blend of traditional and modern cooking on an old plantation. *Ste-Anne (tel: 87 32 03).*

MARTINIQUE

La Lafayette $$
French–Creole food in a restaurant overlooking La Savane in the town centre. *Rue de la Liberté, Fort de France (tel: 63 24 09).*

La Grand' Voile $$$
Fresh seafood in a seaside setting. *Pointe du Simon (tel: 70 29 29).*

La Mouina $$$
Creole cuisine on the terrace of an old colonial villa. *Route de la Redoute (tel: 79 34 57).*

MONTSERRAT

Vue Pointe Hotel $$
Popular Wednesday night barbecue in the island's best hotel. *Vue Pointe (tel: 5210).*

Andy's Village Place $
Rock stars used to come here for barbecue chicken and Andy's special sauce. *Salem (tel: 5202).*

NEVIS

Cla-Cha-Del $$
Family run restaurant serving dishes in the home-made style. *Newcastle (tel: 469 9640).*

Looks modest, but Andy's, on Montserrat, has attracted the rich and famous

Miss June's $$$
A sumptuous banquet of island and East Indian cooking. *Stoney Grove Plantation (tel: 469 5330).*

Muriel's Cuisine $$
A traditional taste of the island. *Happy Hill Drive, Charlestown (tel: 469 5920).*

SABA

Captain's Quarters $$$
Elegant dining high above the valley. *Windwardside (tel: 62201).*

ST BARTHELEMY

Guanahani $$$
First-class French cuisine. *Anse du Grand Cul-de-Sac (tel: 27 66 60).*

Bar le Select $
Informal, outdoor eatery in the centre of town. *Gustavia.*

ST EUSTATIUS

Stone Oven $$
Local food and the liveliest place on the island. *Faeshweg (tel: 82247).*

RUM

Rum is the spirit most closely associated with the Caribbean; most visitors will be handed a rum cocktail the moment they check into their hotels. Legend has it that Blackbeard the pirate laced his with a pinch of gunpowder. Whether or not that is true, the drink certainly packs a punch.

By international convention, rum is an alcoholic distillation of fermented sugar cane juice, syrup and/or molasses. It proved the perfect drink for the Caribbean islands, as sugar cane was the key commercial crop for nearly 200 years. This cane used to be cut, bundled and brought to the old wind-driven mills (which can still be seen throughout the islands today). It was then crushed by rollers and the resulting juice was either boiled to produce sugar or distilled into rum. There are two museums of rum, on Guadeloupe and the US Virgins, where traditional methods are demonstrated and antique machinery is on display.

Rums marketed today range from light-bodied blends, suitable for so-called 'dry' drinks, to the rich dark varieties favoured for punches, nogs and frozen cocktails. Most islands have at least one or two commercial varieties, such as Royal Oak in Trinidad, Mount Gay in Barbados, Cavalier in

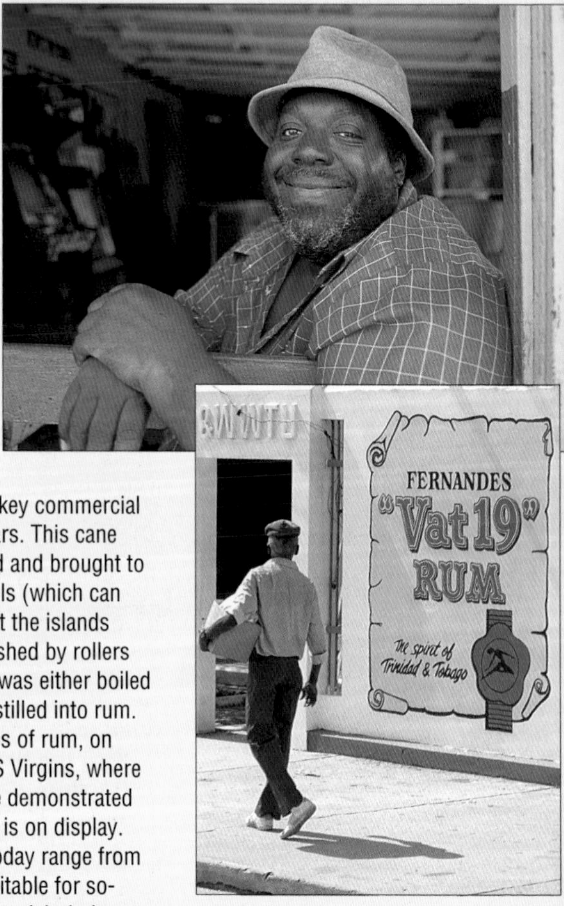

Rum shops come in many shapes and sizes – so does the rum itself

Antigua and Cruzan in the US Virgins. But here and there you may also come across old rum shops where the islanders still sell their own home-made brew, Caveat Emptor.

Several islands have developed distinctive rum-based drinks as after dinner liqueurs. In Barbados they mix rum with cream and call it Crisma; on Saba they mix it with herbs and call it Saba Spice; and on St Maarten/St Martin, for the last 100 years, they have been mixing it with wild berries – it is now bottled commercially and called Guavaberry.

RUM PUNCH

Squeeze a ripe lime into 90gm of good, dark rum and 60gm of sugar syrup; stir well. Add a dash of bitters. Pour this over a glass of ice and grate a little fresh nutmeg on top.

Restaurant on French St Martin

ST KITTS

Chef's Place $$
Kittitian food with cosmopolitan touches. *Church Street Basseterre (tel: 465 6176).*

Ocean Terrace Inn $$
Fine local cuisine on the terrace overlooking the bay. *Basseterre waterfront (tel: 465 2754).*

ST LUCIA

Jimmie's $$
Excellent St Lucian food in a relaxed setting. Highly recommended. *Vigie Cove (tel: 452 5142).*

Green Parrot $$
Famous food and occasional entertainment. *Morne Fortune (tel: 452 3399).*

San Antoine $$
Chic restaurant, with spectacular view of Castries.
Morne Fortune (tel: 452 4660).

Rain $$
Popular meeting place. *Columbus Square, Castries (tel: 452 3022).*

ST MAARTEN/ST MARTIN

Le Bec Fin $$
Romantic setting on the waterfront. *Front Street, Philipsburg (tel: 22976).*

Yvette's Restaurant $$
Authentic Creole cuisine in the former capital of the island. *Quartier d'Orleans (tel: 87 32 03).*

Fish Pot $$
Imaginative cooking with fresh produce and a fine view over the bay. *Grand Case (tel: 87 50 88).*

ST VINCENT AND THE GRENADINES

The French Restaurant $$
Fine dining on a quiet waterfront location. *Villa (tel: 84972).*

Young Island Resort $$$
Good food in a smart private beach resort. *Young Island (tel: 458 4826).*

Frangipani Hotel $$
Friendly service, (amazing nutmeg ice cream), very popular with yachtsmen. *Port Elizabeth, Bequia (tel: 458 3255).*

Basil's Bar $$$
Rub shoulders with the rich and famous in the famous bar on stilts. *Mustique (tel: 458 4621).*

TOBAGO

Store Bay $
An open-air food court near the beach with great Bagonian food. *Store Bay.*

Jemma's Sea View $$
Fine food served in a tree house over the sea. *Speyside (tel: 660 4066).*

TRINIDAD

Café Savanna $$$
Distinctive Trinidadian dishes in a cosy

setting. *Kapok Hotel, Cotton Hill, Port of Spain (tel: 622 6441).*

Veni Mange $$
A small Victorian house where they serve great local food. Book early. *Lucknow Street, St James.*

The Breakfast Shed $
Fast-food island-style by the docks; pick your vendor. *Cruise Ship Harbour, Port of Spain.*

VIRGIN ISLANDS, BRITISH

Mrs Scatliffe's $$
After the island food, the family play island fungi music. *Carrot Bay, Tortola (tel: 495 4556).*

Quito's Gazebo $$
Fish buffets four nights a week plus Quito's own music. *Cane Garden Bay (tel: 495 4639).*

The Last Resort $$
Lavish buffet plus cabaret; a Mecca for yachtsmen in particular. *Beef Island (tel: 495 2520).*

Olde Yard Inn $$
International and local food in friendly surroundings. *The Valley, Virgin Gorda (tel: 495 5544).*

VIRGIN ISLANDS, U.S.

Hotel 1829 $$$
Widely considered to be the best on the island, historic setting. *Government Hill, Charlotte Amalie (tel: 774 1829).*

Blackbeard's Castle $$$
Fantastic views over the city and other islands. *Government Hill, Charlotte Amalie (tel: 776 1234).*

The Old Gallery $
Popular with locals for real, good-value Virgin Island food. *Cruz Bay, St John (tel: 776 7544).*

Fish Trap $$
Over 40 seafood dishes on a covered patio. *Cruz Bay, St John (tel: 776 9817).*

Kendricks $$$
Generous European cooking elegantly served. *Queen Cross Street, Christiansted, St Croix (tel: 773 9199).*

Villa Madeleine $$$
Stylish cuisine in the modern style, hilltop setting. *East End, St Croix (tel: 778 7377).*

Star of the West $
Home cooking in an informal bar by the sea. *Strand Street, Frederiksted, St Croix.*

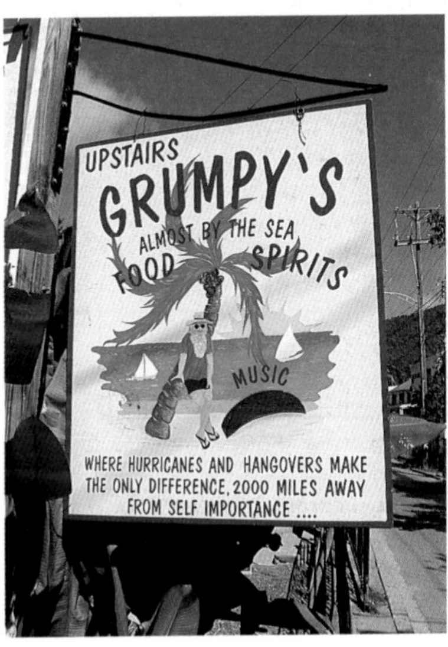

At Cruz Bay, US Virgin Islands

STREET FOOD HYGIENE

The street food of Trinidad and Tobago is superb but it is worth looking for a 'food badge' before you buy. These indicate that the stall has been inspected by the Ministry of Health and has received the seal of approval for hygienic food preparation. This applies to both vendors in town and at the beach.

Hotels and Accommodation

Although holiday brochures tend, almost exclusively, to feature beach resorts, there is in fact a whole range of accommodation options in the Caribbean. It is important to bear in mind that there are two key tourist seasons in the region. From mid-December to mid-April prices almost double as North Americans and Europeans escape their winter. Hotel rooms are at a premium, support services such as car hire companies are particularly busy and hotel staff are often under pressure. Between May and August, however, prices return to normal and the islands are quieter. In between the two seasons, in October and November when most of the rain tends to fall, many of the hotels close their doors for maintenance and staff holidays.

Reservations can be made direct by contacting the hotel by telephone, telex or fax, but most hotels prefer guests to make a reservation through the hotel's representative, a tour operator or a travel agent. State clearly any special requirements, such as the location of the room. Sometimes it is also possible to choose between rooms cooled by air-conditioning and those with ceiling fans. On arrival, if the room does not correspond with what was requested, let

Curtain Bluff Hotel, Antigua

the management know immediately.

Caribbean hotels offer a range of meal options which can be booked in advance. European Plan (EP) means room only, no meals; Continental Plan (CP) includes a Continental breakfast; American Plan (AP) includes a cooked breakfast; Modified American Plan includes breakfast, lunch and dinner. Most hotels are categorised according to a system of stars, although this does not seem to be standardised across the region; a three-star hotel bedroom on one island is often no different from a two-star hotel room on another. Check exactly what is on offer before booking, or to find a tour operator who uses a standardised system for the grading of hotels throughout the region. When calculating the cost of a hotel room remember that many hotels add a mandatory governmment tax and an extra service charge which can increase the bill by as much as 20 per cent.

ALL-INCLUSIVE RESORTS

Increasingly, Caribbean resorts are offering all-inclusive packages which cover all meals and snacks in between, drinks at the bar, cigarettes, watersports, transport to and from town, and even manicures and laundry. Many of these resorts, however, take couples only and will not even allow single people, families or children on to the property.

They are popular with those who like the idea of one payment upfront and no nasty surprises when the final bill appears. However, there is then a temptation to stay on site whereas it is worth remembering that there are many good island restaurants outside the gates of the resort which offer authentic local food, friendly service and memorable experiences.

Ocean View Hotel, Barbados

ACTIVITY AND HEALTH-BASED RESORTS

The combination of sun, sea, sand and sports is a seductive one and several resorts offer inclusive programmes of water and land sports which will appeal to the health-conscious. Other resorts have an emphasis on beauty treatments; perhaps using seaweeds and saltwater, with jetspray wrap and thermal baths. Facial treatments, massages and haircare sessions are also offered.

THOMAS COOK

Traveller's Tip

Travellers who purchase their travel tickets from a Thomas Cook network location are entitled to use the services of any other Thomas Cook network location, free of charge, to make hotel reservations.

NATURE RETREATS

For those who have little interest in the beach and prefer to be closer to nature there are several hotels and centres in unspoilt settings surrounded by tropical birdlife and native bush. They may organise guided nature walks, talks and the opportunity to join in research. Most, however, simply offer a peaceful retreat.

PRIVATE ISLAND RESORTS

Some hotels can be reached only by boat. These are the private island resorts dotted around the Caribbean, but to be found particularly in the Grenadines and the Virgin Islands. The advantages of a tropical island which you may share with only 20 or so other guests, and in luxurious surroundings with first-class service must be weighed against any possible feeling of claustrophobia resulting from being stuck in one place with people you cannot get away from. Most, however, offer a free shuttle service to the nearest main island for shopping and sightseeing.

Nearly every fair-sized hotel has its own pool, as well as the sea

PRIVATE VILLAS AND RENTED HOUSES

There are many properties, often owned by expatriates, which are available for rent and the local tourist offices can supply a list. Some are luxury villas with maid service (and may even include the run of the whole private island), others are simple shacks beside the beach. In the French Antilles there are are also a large number of family-owned gîtes for rent on a daily, weekly or monthly basis, organised by the local Syndicats d'Initiative.

The location and amenities are very important when choosing rented accommodation; while a town house in the suburbs may be suitable for someone eager to explore Port of Spain, a villa with a pool close to the beach may well be better for a family with children. Whichever option is chosen, self catering can be expensive. Most of the supermarket goods that are familiar to tourists have been imported from Europe or North America and the price is likely to reflect this. It is usually cheaper to shop for produce in the local fish, fruit and vegetable markets.

Getaway resort – Young Island

GUESTHOUSES

Staying with a family is not only cheaper than living in a hotel, it can also be a way of getting to know an island better while making new friends. Guesthouses tend to be smaller properties – probably with no more than six or eight rooms – and may well provide a second source of income for the family. They may offer just bed and breakfast, or dinner might be included as well; but home-cooked meals are likely to include local dishes and, even if they are not always taken with the family, will usually be enjoyed with fellow guests. The personal touch is the main attraction here, someone to offer advice and practical details about your stay on the island.

A list of approved guesthouses is usually available from the island tourist offices.

On the French islands the organised system of Relais is similar to that on mainland France, where the visitor stays in centrally approved, and often very comfortable, family-run accommodation and eats *table d'hôte*.

HISTORIC HOUSES

Some hotels have the added attraction of a little bit of history. They may be famous old plantation houses, castles or pirate strongholds, or they may once have been the homes of royalty or celebrated politicians. Without exception they offer agreeable, if expensive, lodgings. Contact island tourist offices for a list of their most historic hotels.

On Business

While it used to be considered purely a holiday destination, over the last few years the eastern Caribbean has immeasurably improved its facilities for the business sector. The local tourist bureaux (see page 189) or their representatives abroad will supply a detailed list of facilities available. Some have presentation packs dedicated to the business traveller.

ACCOMMODATION AND CONFERENCE FACILITIES

Most hotels have meeting rooms which can be hired for the day and an increasing number are building conference facilities – even on some of the smaller islands such as Montserrat. The larger islands have purpose-built international conference centres, with air-conditioning, film, slide and over-head projectors, lecterns, and sound-amplification equipment.

The University of the West Indies – divided by faculty between several different islands in the region – has conference and meeting facilities on campus, as well as accommodation in halls of residence (depending on the time of year). All the large hotels have banqueting facilities capable of coping with a large group of business people, whether it requires a cocktail party, a finger buffet or a full five-course dinner; often theme nights (Pirates' Parties, Buccaneers' Nights) can be arranged, which include island cuisine and entertainment such as limbo dancing.

Office block overlooking the Bridgetown harbour, Barbados

BUSINESS ETIQUETTE

This is influenced by both European and North American practices, although the Caribbean ambience leads to a more relaxed dress code (for example, short-sleeved shirts are common and ties are often dispensed with). However, although time-keeping is often lax in other areas of Caribbean life, lateness is usually frowned upon in business circles. The business lunch is alive and well in the Caribbean and it is common practice to invite business associates to dinner in the evening in island restaurants.

BUSINESS HOURS

These vary from island to island but, in general, the business day starts early in the Caribbean, with most people at their desks by 8.30am at the latest. A lunch hour is usually taken and offices tend to close by 5pm. If Saturday is worked, it is usually a half day.

COMMUNICATIONS

Direct dial international telephone calls are easily made from hotel bedrooms or from public call boxes in towns and at airports using a prepaid telephone card. Occasionally, mobile cellular telephones are available for hire by the day or the week (particularly on those islands with a strong yacht charter connection).

Fax machines are available at hotel receptions but the management may charge a fee for a fax received as well as a fax sent. Telex, telegram and fax facilities tend to be cheaper from each island's main telecommunications office. International mail services tend to be slow, but some of the larger islands operate express business mail services. Satellite networks now mean many hotels offer an international news service.

SECRETARIAL AND LEGAL SERVICES

There are offices in virtually every Caribbean town offering secretarial, short-hand and word-processing services by the hour, day or week. These companies will also co-ordinate conferences, book airline charters and photographers and organise entertainments and sightseeing trips for groups and individuals. Those hotels which have secretarial staff can also be called upon to provide typing and word-processing.

Every island has solicitors willing, for a fee, to advise the visiting business person on the finer points of island law. Often they are listed in the local Yellow Pages.

Chartered helicopter is a quick but expensive mode of travel between the islands

TRANSLATION SERVICES

Most people speak English in the eastern Caribbean, including on the Dutch islands of Saba, St Eustatius and St Maarten/St Martin. Translation services are available, however, on the French islands, in the main population centres as well as at hotels. Some international telephone networks, such as AT&T, have 24-hour language-line services.

Practical Guide

CONTENTS

ARRIVING

Most islands require a valid passport for entry, although US citizens usually need show only proof of identity. Visas are seldom required except for the US islands. However, non-US citizens arriving in the US Virgin Islands do not require a visa if their home country is a member of the US Visa Waiver programme (for example, UK). Visitors from South Africa will need a visa.

Immigration forms are generally distributed on board aircraft or ships before arrival. They should be handed to the immigration officer on arrival, together with your passport. The stamp on the passport usually indicates the maximum permitted stay on the island and emphasises that no work should be sought or undertaken.

By Air

Bridgetown, Barbados, and San Juan, Puerto Rico, are the major international entry points into the eastern Caribbean. Facilities at Bridgetown generally stay open until the last departure of the day. They include catering outlets, a bank, a post office and shops. Flight enquiry number is 428 7107 ext 4605 (available 8am–10pm). The taxi journey to the city is 30 minutes. There is also a bus service which takes only 15 minutes longer and is much cheaper.

THOMAS COOK
Traveller's Tip

Any Thomas Cook Network location will offer airline ticket re-routing and revalidation free of charge to MasterCard cardholders and to travellers who have purchased their travel tickets from Thomas Cook.

Most Caribbean airports have tourist information desks which advise on ground transport and taxi fares.

Bus services from Caribbean airports are very rare; taking a taxi is usually the sole option for the independent traveller. However, every island has a list of agreed taxi fares for the journey between the airport and principal destinations.

Departure

It is important, particularly if travelling to some of the smaller islands, to reconfirm the next stage of the journey as soon as possible. This can be done at the airline office at the airport.

CAMPING

There are few facilities for camping. Only the French islands and the Virgin Islands have approved sites.

WEATHER CONVERSION CHART

25.4mm = 1 inch

°F = 1.8 × °C + 32

CHILDREN

The larger modern resorts have good facilities for children, including babysitting services, clubs and special menus. Care should be taken to protect children from the sun with high-factor sun cream, even on cloudy days. Nappies and baby food are available in supermarkets and pharmacies.

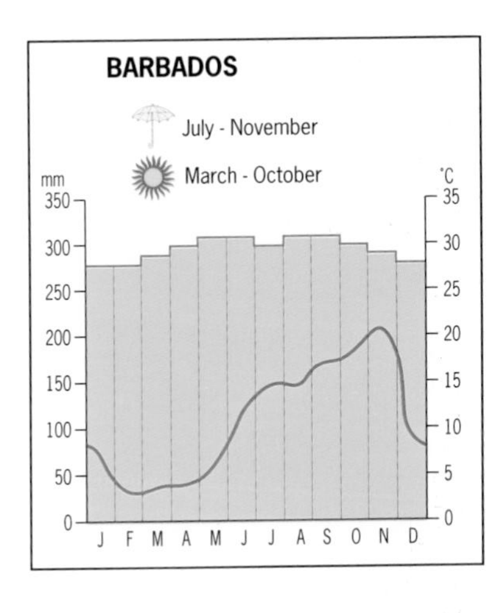

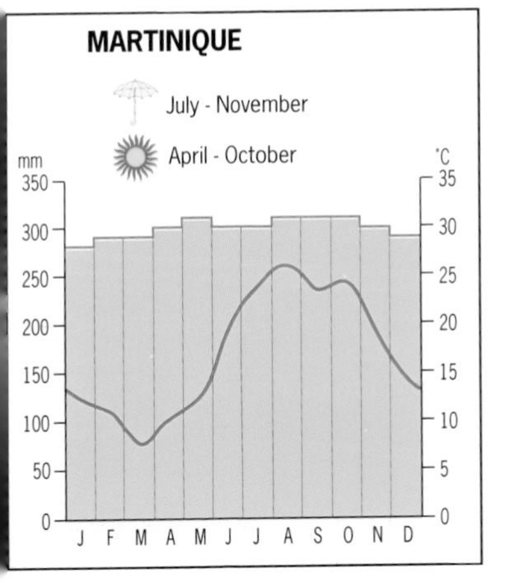

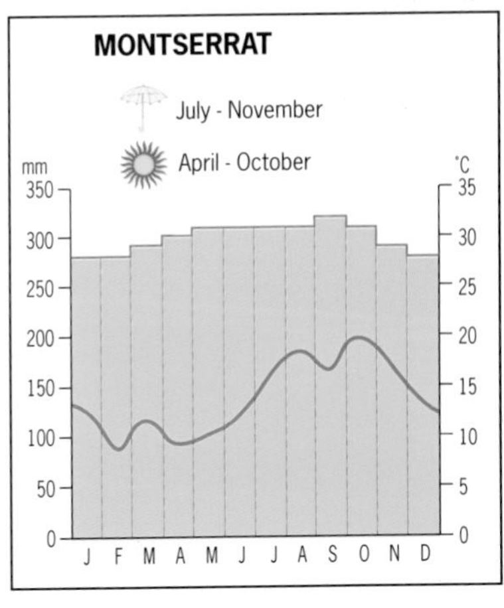

Conversion Table

FROM	TO	MULTIPLY BY
Inches	Centimetres	2.54
Feet	Metres	0.3048
Yards	Metres	0.9144
Miles	Kilometres	1.6090
Acres	Hectares	0.4047
Gallons	Litres	4.5460
Ounces	Grams	28.35
Pounds	Grams	453.6
Pounds	Kilograms	0.4536
Tons	Tonnes	1.0160

To convert back, for example from centimetres to inches, divide by the number in the the third column.

Men's Suits

UK	36	38	40	42	44	46	48
Rest of Europe	46	48	50	52	54	56	58
US	36	38	40	42	44	46	48

Dress Sizes

UK	8	10	12	14	16	18
France	36	38	40	42	44	46
Italy	38	40	42	44	46	48
Rest of Europe	34	36	38	40	42	44
US	6	8	10	12	14	16

Men's Shirts

UK	14	14.5	15	15.5	16	16.5	17
Rest of Europe	36	37	38	39/40	41	42	43
US	14	14.5	15	15.5	16	16.5	17

Men's Shoes

UK	7	7.5	8.5	9.5	10.5	11
Rest of Europe	41	42	43	44	45	46
US	8	8.5	9.5	10.5	11.5	12

Women's Shoes

UK	4.5	5	5.5	6	6.5	7
Rest of Europe	38	38	39	39	40	41
US	6	6.5	7	7.5	8	8.5

CLIMATE

Year-round day-time temperatures average between 27°–29°C with the thermometer dropping to 15°–18°C at night. Often there are cooling trade winds to temper the heat of the day. The driest time of year is from December to April or May. Rainfall is generally heaviest during October and November (though June is wetter in Trinidad and Tobago). Hurricanes hardly ever happen, but when they do it is generally between the end of August and October.

CRIME

Crime is rare on the smaller islands but do not put temptation in the way of petty thieves. Lock cars, put valuables in the hotel safe and keep money out of sight. On the larger islands, particularly St Thomas and Trinidad, avoid walking in unlit or quiet streets or on deserted beaches at night.

CUSTOMS REGULATIONS

The amount travellers can bring into each island varies. A general rule of thumb would be about 1 litre of spirits, 200 cigarettes, and any personal effects and amount of money a tourist would reasonably use while on the island.

DEPARTURE TAX

Most islands levy a departure tax at the airport when you are leaving: some islands will accept US dollars instead of local currency. The actual sum varies between islands and tends to increase at regular intervals. It is best to check the exact sum required in advance.

DISABLED TRAVELLERS

Careful planning is required by the disabled traveller, for there are few facilities for these visitors in the eastern

Caribbean. Large modern resorts may have rooms adapted for disabled use, but most hotels do not. Roads and pavements are frequently rutted and uneven and ease of access to restaurants should be established when booking.

DRIVING

While a valid national, and occasionally international, driving licence is required, many islands also demand that the visitor buys a local licence. This can be obtained either from a police station or a car hire company.

Car hire insurance usually offers a Collision Damage Waiver. However, it is quite common on some islands to find there is a limited liability clause instead, for example up to the first US$1000 of the damage.

It is important to drive defensively and to expect the unexpected. Drivers often stop in the middle of the road to talk to each other. Large potholes appear around every corner.

In the event of breakdown, hire companies issue a phone number to summon assistance. Although there are frequent petrol stations on all islands, it is a good idea to fill up before a long, round-island tour.

ELECTRICITY

On most islands covered in this book the electricity supply is 220 volts. However, on some, notably the US Virgins, it is 100–120 volts. Some islands even have the two different systems running simultaneously. Check with the hotel concierge or tourist office.

EMBASSIES

Every island state or principal island of a group, for example St Kitts or Guadeloupe, will have an embassy or consulate representing the nations of that island's main tourist visitors.

EMERGENCY TELEPHONE NUMBERS

These telephone numbers are in the process of being standardised. Make sure you check the relevant numbers on arrival.

Anguilla Police: 2333; Ambulance: 2551
Antigua Police: 462 0125; Ambulance: 0251
Barbados Police: 112; Ambulance: 115
Dominica Police and Ambulance: 999
Grenada Police: 911; Ambulance: 434
Guadeloupe Police: 17; Ambulance: 82 89 33
Martinique Police: 17; Ambulance: 71 59 48
Montserrat Police: 999; Ambulance: 911
Saba Police: 63237; Ambulance: 63288
St Barthélemy Police: 27 66 66; Ambulance: 276085
St Eustatius Police: 82333; Ambulance: 82211
St Kitts and St Nevis Police and Ambulance: 911
St Lucia Police and Ambulance: 999
St Maarten Police: 22222; Ambulance: 22111
St Martin Police: 17; Ambulance: 18
St Vincent Police and Ambulance: 999
Trinidad and Tobago Police: 999; Ambulance: 990
Virgin Islands, British Police and Ambulance: 999
Virgin Islands, U.S. Police: 915; Ambulance: 922

Thomas Cook travellers' cheque refund (24-hour service – report loss or theft within 24 hours): +1 609 987 7300 (reverse charges/collect call).

Getting a tan is fine, but sunburn can make you seriously ill

ETIQUETTE

Topless bathing is forbidden on all except the French islands. In towns and villages it is advisable to dress conservatively; skimpy shorts, bikinis and bare chests often offend. It is generally considered rude to ask an islander a question (even to ask directions) without making a friendly greeting first. Jackets and ties are seldom required by holiday-makers in the Caribbean.

HEALTH

There are no mandatory health requirements for the tourist to the Caribbean but a certificate of immunisation against yellow fever may be required if arriving from an infected area.

Immunisation against typhoid, polio and tetanus is recommended, and hepatitis A should be added to the list if you are likely to be staying outside established tourist areas. If you are staying for more than a week or two anywhere in the eastern Caribbean, you should consider also hepatitis B and rabies vaccinations. Like everywhere in the world, AIDS is present.

In the whole of the region drink only bottled water and take common-sense precautions over food and drink. Beware of spiny sea urchins, coral and jellyfish.

Hospital facilities are generally good, although the smaller islands are ill-equipped to deal with very complex cases. Proper health insurance is vital – particularly for the American islands where medical care can be particularly expensive – and should be purchased before travel. All hotels will arrange an English-speaking doctor to visit. However, adequate supplies of the visitor's usual medications should be carried in case they are not available from island pharmacies.

MACHINEEL TREE

Beware of the machineel tree. It is found on the coast of most islands and its fruit looks like little green apples. These are poisonous. Do not even shelter from the rain under these trees as the water running off the leaves can cause nasty blisters. Often it is marked by a broad red stripe painted round the trunk.

HITCH-HIKING

Hitch-hiking is unusual in the Caribbean, except on the French islands. However, it is common when walking on smaller islands to be offered a lift by a passing car and a careful judgement is required whether to accept or not. In most cases it will simply be a friendly gesture.

INSECT LIFE

Although most hotels in infested areas spray their grounds to get rid of mosquitoes, biting insects can still be an enormous irritant, particularly at night. There is an especially annoying form of sand fly known colloquially as a 'no-see-um', which hangs around beaches. The best idea is to be prepared in advance, with an effective insect spray which can be used on all areas of exposed skin before going out at night. Malaria is not endemic to this region.

LOST PROPERTY

In the event of loss, enquiries should be made at the nearest hotel or public building. If the property is not found, a report should be obtained from the local police station for any insurance claim.

MAPS

There are few really detailed maps of the smaller islands, but plenty of perfectly adequate, more general maps. There are many free publications available from hotels and tourist offices which include maps and directions to the main tourist sights and destinations. Nautical charts tend to be more detailed and are available through island yacht clubs.

MEDIA

Every island has at least one daily newspaper with a page devoted to international news. In addition to local radio and television stations, islands increasingly have American-influenced cable networks with a variety of channels. Check with the hotel concierge or local press.

MONEY MATTERS

The main island currencies are the eastern Carribean dollar, the French franc, the Dutch guilder, the Trinidad and Tobago dollar and the American dollar, depending on the island. The eastern Caribbean dollar and the Trinidad and Tobago dollar have a fixed exchange rate with the US dollar. On all islands traders generally accept the US dollar in lieu of local currency; it is important, however, that when a price is quoted in dollars, it is clear whether the price refers to US dollars or local currency.

Travellers' cheques are used widely to free tourists from the hazards of carrying large amounts of cash; often, in the event of loss or theft, they can be quickly refunded with the aid of an emergency telephone number. Although some countries accept other denominations (for example, sterling in the former British West Indies, French francs in the French Antilles), Thomas Cook recommend US dollar cheques. These can frequently be used to settle bills in major hotels, larger restaurants and tourist shops without the need to cash them first.

There are banks on all the islands, but service can be extremely slow; to avoid wasting time check which queue is for which service. Banking hours vary by island but, as a general rule, it is better to go as early in the day as possible and to avoid the lunchtime rush. Most major credit cards are accepted at hotels and restaurants, but few cash dispenser machines work with international cards.

The following member companies of the Thomas Cook Worldwide Network can provide emergency assistance in the event of loss or theft of Thomas Cook MasterCard travellers' cheques: Alexander Parrish Ltd, Thames Street, St Johns, Antigua; Paul Foster Travel, Erin Court, Bishop's Court Hill, Collvmore Rock, St Michael, Bridgetown, Barbados; International Travel Ltd, Transnational Building, West Bay Road, Grand Cayman; Mussons Trading Ltd, Dorset House, Old Street, Roseau, Dominica.

ORGANISED TOURS

The hotel concierge usually has information on island tours; if not the tourist office. Although these do not offer the freedom of a hired car they do have the advantage of knowledgeable local guides.

Antigua

Alexander Parrish (Antigua) Ltd, Thames Street, St John's: services include car hire, local tours, tours to nearby islands.

St Lucia

Sunlink International, Castries: services include local tours and tours to the Grenadines, Mustique, Martinique, Barbados and Dominica.

Barbados

Chalene Tours Ltd, Salem Street, Lawrence Gap: services include local tours and car hire, tours to other islands and cruises.

An echo from Britain on Antigua

The Thomas Cook Network members listed on page 187 all offer organised tours.

PHARMACIES

Pharmacies are plentiful and familiar brand-named drugs are on display. Always check the date stamp before buying. A good range of modern toiletries is available, along with remedies for the most common island ailments (including sunburn lotions). Few islands have emergency pharmaceutical provision beyond hospital and doctor services.

PHOTOGRAPHY

Take a good supply of film as film stored in island shops may have been affected by the heat and it may also be old stock. The best photographs are generally taken early or late in the day, as the midday sun throws harsh shadows.

TELEPHONES

Generally, the telephone network is very good in the Caribbean. In addition to coin boxes, every island uses a system of telephone cards which can be bought for various values at post offices and in some shops, and which can be used to make international calls. Long-distance calls can be made from hotel rooms but a service charge will normally be added to the bill. The Boatphone Company has credit card cellular telephones in several locations but while these are convenient they tend to be extremely expensive. On the French islands some extra wide telephone kiosks have been adapted for wheelchair users.

TIME

The eastern Caribbean is four hours behind Grenwich Mean Time and one hour ahead of Eastern Standard Time.

TIPPING

Although hotel and restaurant bills often include a service charge, tips are increasingly expected by staff on the islands. As a general rule, if you wish to reward good service, US$1, or the local equivalent, per piece of luggage is acceptable for hotel porters, and 10 per cent should be adequate for taxi drivers and staff in restaurants.

TOILETS

Public toilets are scarce in the Caribbean, although they may be found near popular tourist sites. However, most hotels and bars will allow visitors to use their facilities even if they are not patrons or guests. Where there are toilets on the French islands, they are often supervised, and it is customary to leave a tip.

TOURIST OFFICES

These are generally very helpful and a good source of free literature. Staff will be able to advise on routes for excursions and can make restaurant bookings. The main offices on each island are as follows:

Anguilla, The Valley (tel: 2759).
Antigua and Barbuda, Thanes Street, St John's (tel: 462 0480).
Barbados, Harbour Road, Bridgetown (tel: 427 2623).
Dominica, Valley Road, Roseau (tel: 82045).
Guadeloupe, Square de la Banque, Pointe-à-Pitre (tel: 82 24 83).
Grenada, The Carenage, St George's (tel: 440 2279).
Martinique, Bord de la Mer, Fort-de-France (tel: 63 79 60).
Montserrat, Church Road, Plymouth (tel: 2230).
Nevis, DRWalwyn Plaza, Charlestown (tel: 469 5521).
Saba, Windwardside (tel: 62231).
St Barthélemy, Rue Auguste Nyman, Gustavia (tel: 27 60 08).
St Eustatius, Upper Town, Oranjestad (tel: 82433).
St Kitts, Pelican Mall, Basseterre (tel: 465 2620).
St Lucia, Pointe Seraphine (tel: 453 0053).
St Maarten, De Ruyterplein, Philipsburg (tel: 22337).
St Martin, Port de Marigot (tel: 87.53.26).
St Vincent, Finance Complex, Kingstown (tel: 71502).
Tobago, Scarborough Mall (tel: 639 2125).
Trinidad, 134 Frederick Street, Port of Spain (tel: 623 1932).
Virgin Islands (British), Road Town, Tortola (tel: 494 3134).
Virgin Islands (U.S), The Waterfront, Charlotte Amalie, St Thomas (tel: 774 8784); and Old Customs Scalehouse, Christiansted St Croix (tel: 773 0495).

Most of the larger islands are also represented by tourist offices in cities abroad (eg New York, London, Paris). These offices will provide information and advice on your trip in advance of departure.

ACKNOWLEDGEMENTS
The Automobile Association wishes to thank the following organisations, libraries and photographers for their assistance in the preparation of this book.

ALLSPORT UK LTD 162 (B Radford)
ARDEA LONDON 127 (M D England)
SOPHIE CAMPBELL 113a
JAMES HENDERSON 11, 27, 28, 31b, 38, 39, 40, 41b, 42, 43, 44, 45, 82, 99, 108, 110, 111, 119, 131, 158, 165b, 180
INTERNATIONAL PHOTOBANK 1, 49, 86b, 109, 141, 147
NATURE PHOTOGRAPHERS LTD 70a, 71a, 71b (P R Sterry), 113b (S C Bisserot)
SPECTRUM COLOUR LIBRARY 91, 97a, 156
ZEFA PICTURE LIBRARY (UK) LTD 78, 112, 156/7, 157a, 157b, 167
US VIRGIN ISLANDS DIVISION OF TOURISM 23, 159

The remaining photographs are held in the AA Photo Library and were taken by Peter Baker with the exception of the inset which was taken by Roy Victor.

The Automobile Association would also like to thank the following people and companies for their help in the making of this book: Sandridge Beach Hotel, Barbados; Mr Michael Starr, Alexander Parrish Ltd, Antigua; Mr Charles Gloumeau, Chalene Tours, Barbados; Ms Linda Gray, Sunlink International, St Lucia; Ms Pauline Barnard, St Lucia Representative Services Ltd.
The author would like to thank the tourist offices on all the islands covered by this book, their island headquarters and their London offices. Also LIAT, Air France and American Airlines.

Series adviser: Melissa Shales

Copy editor: Sally Knowles